BIBLE AND PRACTICE

BRITISH LIBERATION THEOLOGY
Series Editors: Chris Rowland and John Vincent

1. LIBERATION THEOLOGY UK

2. GOSPEL FROM THE CITY

3. LIBERATION SPIRITUALITY

4. BIBLE AND PRACTICE

In Preparation

5. THEOLOGIES FROM PRACTICE

6. TO BE ANNOUNCED

British Liberation Theology is published under the auspices of the British Liberation Theology Project, the Institute for British Liberation Theology of the Urban Theology Unit and the Las Casas Network. The Management Group of the British Liberation Theology Project is: Rev Inderjit Bhogal, Dr Andrew Bradstock, Bishop Laurie Green, Prof. Christopher Rowland, Ms Bridget Rees, Mr Mike Simpson, Dr. John Vincent and Sister Margaret Walsh. Bridget Rees and John Vincent are Joint Co-ordinators.

The annual volumes of British Liberation Theology are available on subscription or as single books. Single copies may be obtained price £7.50, p&p 85p. Volumes 4, 5 & 6 are obtainable on subscription for £20 inc. p & p. All three of the first volumes (1,2 and 3) can be obtained price £15 inc. p&p. Normal discounts (35%) are available to booksellers. Quantities of 20 or over are available to other organisations at a special discount (25%). Cheques to URBAN THEOLOGY UNIT.

Address all enquiries to: Janet Ayres, Support Services Manager, URBAN THEOLOGY UNIT, 210 Abbeyfield Road, Sheffield, S4 7AZ.

BRITISH LIBERATION THEOLOGY 4

BIBLE AND PRACTICE

Edited by
CHRIS ROWLAND
and
JOHN VINCENT

Sheffield
URBAN THEOLOGY UNIT

ISBN: 0 907490 09 3

Urban Theology Unit is Registered Charity No. 505334

URBAN THEOLOGY UNIT
210 Abbeyfield Road
Sheffield
S4 7AZ

Sub-edited and Typeset by Debbie Herring at the Urban Theology Unit.

Printed by Pemberley Printers, Attercliffe, Sheffield

CONTENTS

6

7

EDITORIAL NOTE

BRITISH LIBERATION THEOLOGY is the overall title for a series of Bi-annual Volumes, designed to bring together new writing in the UK, using the methods of Liberation Theology, and recording the practice and spirituality of people involved in liberation struggles in Britain.

LIBERATION THEOLOGY UK was the first volume, intended to set the scene for a British Liberation Theology within the wider context of world-wide liberation theologies, and to indicate some of the ways in which liberation theology has worked and is working in contemporary thinking and discipleship. The level of the chapters in the volume was intentionally academic and pastoral. It shows how British theologies of liberation both see themselves alongside those of other continents, and also pursue distinctive indigenous agendas.

The following volumes begin at the other end – the levels specifically of pastoral and popular practice. The second volume, GOSPEL FROM THE CITY, contains the stories, the theology and the spirituality of several contemporary disciples and groups, who see themselves as putting into practice or being motivated by liberation theology. They are stories of the practice of liberation in the urban scene today.

The third volume, LIBERATION SPIRITUALITY, records some practice and reflection in terms of lifestyle, discipleship, and prayer which are found among liberation-style practitioners. Several contributors also reflect on the personal and corporate practice of Liberation Theology in Britain, and discern some significant elements and some emerging characteristics.

This fourth volume, BIBLE AND PRACTICE, records stories of the practice of Liberation Theology activists who use the Bible in a variety of ways, and also articles on specific aspects of the Bible, by biblical scholars and pastoral workers. The essays indicate the variety of ways in which the Bible functions in Liberation Practice – but also how common methodologies are emerging from different locations and usages.

The fifth volume we plan to be on THEOLOGIES FROM PRACTICE, in which representatives of the wide spectrum of contemporary liberation-style practitioners utilise and extend the models and meanings of Christian faith.

In the main, as heretofore, the work of specific "branches" of liberation theologies goes on primarily elsewhere – Feminist Theology, Black Theology, Regional Theologies, Lesbian and Gay Theologies, Womanist Theology. We have no wish to presume to "take over" the whole scene, though we do hope to have chapters or possibly volumes which reflect these growing and productive areas in which liberation theology proceeds from the stand-point of particular groups. Indeed, it might be that our effort will encourage them also to wider publication. Of course, that would certainly not be the case for Feminist Theology, which has already created highly significant developments, and which has certainly blazed the trail both for a more general liberation theology, and also for liberation theologies from the stand-points of the women and men oppressed in other ways.

We hope at various times to include theological discussions concerning the wider theological debates on Britain, and the legitimacy or appropriateness of British liberation theologies, especially taking into account the use made of liberation theology perspectives in other contemporary British theologians. But there has been a tendency to discuss such matters in abstract fashion – witness the endless papers, articles and chapters on the theme "What is the relevance of liberation theology to British Christians/Churches/Theology?" It may be a useful change to postpone such theoretical questions for a few years, and let some of those who want to work this way get on and see what they can produce.

We would like to invite readers to offer contributions (3,000-6,000 words). Later volumes may cover biblical theology, political theology, and practical issues in personal, community, political and public life, from liberation theology viewpoints. Please address enquiries to either of us:

CHRIS ROWLAND
Queen's College, Oxford, OX1 4AW

JOHN VINCENT
Urban Theology Unit, Sheffield, S4 7AZ

June 2001

Chris Rowland, Bridget Rees, and Ruth Weston

PRACTICAL EXEGESIS IN CONTEXT

1. Participation versus learning

This article contains the report of a Bible study which formed part of the summer school on Bible and Practice at the Urban Theology Unit in Sheffield in 1999. It is preceded and concluded with reflections on the process of participative Bible study in general and on this occasion in particular.

Throughout this exercise (and it was something which was more an issue for Chris than others) was the feeling, on the basis of previous difficult experiences, that those whose 'names' had been advertised on the list (professors rather than participants, therefore!) needed to provide something more than a role as facilitators of a process. So, there was compromise in the extent of the participative method adopted, in that a sketch of one theme from the gospel, echoing material from David Rensberger's approach to John 3 and 9 in his book *Overcoming the World*, formed part of the preparatory work for the group exercise and acted as a catalyst for those discussions [1].

There is an ongoing issue here which affects those who are committed to the practice of adult education methods inside and outside the academy. Bitter experience has been that those who come to a session organised by a professor want input in a lecture form, and do not want to be 'facilitated' in any kind of participative way. They do not want to be part of a learning process in which the input of the 'expert' is more to do with method than content, at least in the first instance. To be fair to friends at the UTU in 1999 and on other occasions, this may not have been so important for them, as their desire for engagement and participation makes clear. Nevertheless experience prior to the UTU meeting (and since) has suggested that learning processes in which a professor facilitates and enables rather than lectures sets up significant levels of disappointment. Participative classes are never deemed to be good enough. There is a strong desire to sit at the feet of the expert, even if the reaction to the expert may be negative. This is an ongoing issue in adult education, which is particularly poignant for those of us in institutions of higher education: there is a resistance to good learning in a group, in which there is a co-operative and participative spirit, and the fantasy persists that good learning only goes on when the expert sets out the material before one. This is a particular problem for the interpretation of the Bible, as we shall see.

One of the features of theology since the Reformation has been the enormous industry that has been devoted to the interpretation of Scripture, as in the words of this text there is to be found the very voice of God. So the devotion to these texts of the best of human endeavour is both a sign of respect and a key to understanding the voice of God. Much modern biblical study is an inheritor of the Reformation's emphasis on the words as the primary witness to the ways of God. It matters to devote attention to them, their contexts and their original meaning, for thereby one may discern the voice of God who has chosen to reveal God's self through these particular words and these particular authors at a particular time and place. That has required a group of people, who will not only translate and provide the words in an accessible form, but, as has happened in modern biblical interpretation, offer the proper way of approaching these words, thereby guaranteeing that the knowledge of the divine that comes through the study of Scripture is rightly discerned. Such attentiveness to minute detail has not always been the sine qua non of scriptural study, nor is it in the modern world. In earlier centuries we find a less methodical, more oblique, and less analytical, approach to the Scriptures, in which devotion to the text for its own sake is rare. Rather, the text functions as a tool to enable a meeting with and understanding of the divine will, guided by the fellowship of Christians under the inspiration of the Holy Spirit.

For many modern exegetes, study of the meaning of an ancient text must be the essential prerequisite before the exegete embarks on contemporary application. Exegesis involves two steps, therefore, understanding and interpretation, the former being a dispassionate affair arising from the detached study of the Scriptures, devoid of any contemporary 'issues' which may (unhelpfully it is supposed) affect the exegete, the latter allowing these issues to intrude as a necessary contribution to the interpretative process. This kind of approach (with all that this involves in terms of 'reading in' via illustrative parallels or the insight of experience) is always going to be an experimental affair, which will rarely be a detached matter.[2]

The position of mainstream exegetes is one that many liberation theologians (among others) would want to dispute. They do so for several reasons. Firstly, the approach of interpretation and application may be neat and tidy in theory but masks the extent to which in 'historical exegesis' contemporary issues motivate the agenda [3]. Secondly, they believe that understanding of a text is enhanced by the process of application. To put it simply: how you live or act conditions the way in which you understand. In other words, the practice of the life of discipleship and the context in which that discipleship takes place throw up understandings of texts which would only with difficulty have emerged in the calm reflection of academy or church. It is not that the 'action-reflection' model is invariably going to offer the right meaning of a text, but it does at least lay on us an obligation to take such insight with as much seriousness as we might the effusions of one who is recognised as an expert in exegesis. The implication of the liberationist perspective is that academic endeavour might not, in some instances at least, offer us the best or most appropriate understanding of a text, and that one who is engaged in working out the meaning of the text for today might often capture the spirit of the text better.

2. See, Judge and Act

Carlos Mesters has worked as an exegete with base ecclesial communities (CEB's) in Brazil for the last thirty years. The detail of his approach cannot be neatly encapsulated. His pamphlets cover many of the books of the Bible and vary in their interpretative approach. Mesters has suggested that 'life' or 'reality' is just as important as the text of Scripture and he compares the way in which the Bible has been discovered and used with the way in which the bible was used in the patristic period [4]. The text becomes a catalyst in the exploration of pressing contemporary issues relevant to the community; it offers a language to articulate contemporary concerns and help the understanding of them. There is an immediacy in the way in which the text is used. A different way of reading the text has arisen. Its emphasis is on the method: **see** (starting where one is with one's experience, which for the majority in Latin America means an experience of poverty), **judge** (understanding the reasons for that kind of existence and relating them to the story of the deliverance from oppression in the Bible) and **act**. With this approach, ordinary people have taken the Bible into their own hands and begun to read the word of God in the circumstances of their existence, but also in comparison with the stories of the people of God in other times and other places, and have discovered an ally in the story of the people of God in the scriptures.

Many liberation theologians, like Mesters, spend a significant part of each week working with grass roots communities in the shanty towns on the periphery of large cities or in rural communities. As part of their pastoral work they listen and help the process of reflection on the Bible which is going on the grassroots communities. Their writing has not taken place in the context of academic institutions which have rendered them immune from the personal and social pressures of the countries in which they live. It is that experience of identification with the poor and involvement pastorally in their struggles which is the motivating force driving their theology. Mesters suggests that what is happening in this way of reading the Bible is in fact a rediscovery of the older methods of interpretation which stress the priority of the spirit of the word rather than its letter. God speaks through life; but that word is one that is illuminated by the Bible: 'the principal objective of reading the Bible is not to interpret the bible but to interpret life with the help of the Bible'. Such a situation permits those whom Gerald West terms 'ordinary readers' to discover meaning which can so easily elude the technically better equipped exegete [5].

Enabling the poor to engage with the Bible has involved a programme of education of the contents of the biblical material so that it can be a resource for thousands who cannot read. Popular education material often relates stories told within the Basic Communities. Groups start with familiar stories from life, as many Christians feel that the biblical text is far too sacred for them to be interacting with it, particularly when it come to relating its words to the rough and tumble of ordinary life. For example, in the São Paulo Bible study series, *Parabolas de Hoje*, after the short slide sequence a group is asked to discuss a story told by a community. They should recall similar experiences, identify with various members of the story and share what their feelings might have been. It is only at another, later, meeting that the biblical text is introduced and discussed, and a comparison made with the story from the everyday life of a poor community. At the end of the process, a commentary prepared by the exegetical experts is read and discussed, and any further insights drawn from the reflection which relate to the present call to discipleship in the community.

There are superficial similarities between this method and the readings of radicals like the early Anabaptists, Winstanley, Bunyan or even Blake (and

13

nearer home in the Bible study packs of 'Unlock')[6]. As it was in early centuries for the protestant radicals, the setting for the reading is a world of poverty, disease and death in which the words of Scripture come to offer hope and a path to life. There is in such developments a return to the methods of lower criticism, which acknowledged the place given to experts in the preparation of the manuscripts and the translations of them, but left the process of interpretation so that a wider group could be included. There is a task needed to give confidence in using the Bible. This is precisely what has happened in a pedagogy in the basic ecclesial communities, where educational material is geared not so much to tell people what the Bible means as to encourage people to *use* the bible, but to do so acknowledging the value of their own experience. This will involve a variety of different techniques ranging from encouraging people to talk and share to simple communication of information of what is in the Bible.

Most conventional are those occasions when some examples are offered of the connections which might be made, possibly involving exegetes themselves who use their expertise to outline what it might have been like for the people of God in another time and place to bear witness as a minority against the weight of the principalities and powers that stood against them. But the resort to the wisdom of contemporary pedagogy, in particular the highly influential methods pioneered by Paulo Freire in his *Pedagogy of the Oppressed*, has enabled a variety of ways of approaching and using the Scriptures which equip people to use them, rather than offering an interpretation ready made to which the only response is to apply what has been handed down by the interpretative experts. Writing about this new situation has the appearance of the trite and superficial as it is impossible adequately to convey in words the particularity and dynamics of a particular piece of interpretative process. One person who has attempted to do this is Gerald West in the grassroots studies he has pioneered in Natal. This has been the subject of several smaller publications and is now discussed in a major contribution to the discussion of the relationship between the academy and the 'ordinary readers' [7].

3. Setting the Scene

With due appreciation of the difficulties and the contextual nature of any operation, what follows is one example of a Bible Study specifically organised for a particular group of people, all of whom were met to explore a way of reading the Bible which owed much to the liberation theology tradition.

The general outlines of the study session which is now described spanned two periods of about one and a half hours each, including group work. The outlines were discussed in advance, but the actual contours were determined by events of the previous day, in particular a session led by Tim Gorringe on the subject of 'The Bible and Subversion'.[8] In this, Tim drew attention to four issues: the way in which the Bible has been put to different uses; the very different perspectives of different people in different contexts; the recognition of the insights into the injustices of the contemporary world offered by liberationist exegetes; and a query as to whether such insight actually needed the Bible at all. (This latter had been a particular issue for Chris and Tim in their teaching in Oxford. Both had heard presentations by Ched Myers in Oxford, which were stimulating and insightful, but in which Ched had to contend with questions from more sceptical scholars, who, while admiring Myers' political insight, questioned whether the Bible need have any part to play in his analysis of the situation, but should be left to ancient history.)

What provided the basis for the choice of text for the group Bible study during the conference, was the way in which liberationist tradition has in practice worked with its own 'canon within the canon', ignoring key texts, or, say in the case of a book like Exodus, parts of texts. To engage with this issue, the Gospel of John was chosen as one which might offer a test to explore whether the 'spiritual gospel' could inform those who wanted to use the Bible with an avowed awareness of its social context. Alongside this there ran like a thread through this conference an issue which is a pressing one for an occasion of this kind: how do we guarantee that it does not merely replicate the format of the academy, albeit translated to inner city Sheffield? There was emerging in the consultation some resistance to a way of working in which an audience listened to experts. There was some pressure, therefore, to ensure that the method of engagement should reflect the commitment of those gathered for the conference to participative working and the possibility of contextual insight.

4. The Programme

What follows is a report of that occasion in July 1999 including information prepared by one of the groups which engaged in the task. The timetable was:

10.00 - 10.30 Recap of previous day's issues
           Some reflections on John
10.30 – 11.50 individually: one's own situation in the light of John
           pairs : sharing
           groups of 4
11.50 - 12.30 Plenary

The workshop (which, as already indicated, was considerably influenced by a plenary session the night before on the need for more participative approaches) had the following aims which were outlined for the participants at the beginning of the Bible study:

Overall Aim
- to share experience of relating Bible to practice, the insights we've gained and the problems we've faced.
- to provide material which can be the basis for an article for a future British Liberation Theology volume on the Bible and Practice.
- to use a text which may not be one that we'd often use, namely the Gospel of John.
- to make ourselves find out whether there is radical potential in Biblical texts.

The task for the participants was set up as follows
- To think of a situation and use John to reflect on it.
- To ask, What new perspectives did you have on your situation? What new perspectives did you have on John?
- if you've found it impossible to use John, suggest why John proved to be so difficult.
- as you go about your task, ask yourselves what criteria you would use to judge whether a text is liberative.
- To write up your report concisely and clearly (this is what I shall be working with as I seek to put the article together)

Throughout the group sessions Tim Gorringe and I were available to offer any theological resources. It was made quite clear that our expertise was there to help deal with problems of interpretation which the groups themselves had come up with. As far as the method was concerned, the time was structured to allow the opportunity for individual and corporate reflection. At the start each person was allowed some space to engage with the text and use it to interpret and inform their context.

A way into John's gospel had been offered with a brief sketch of some themes in the gospel, as follows:
THE GOSPEL OF JOHN

The problem
- the individualistic, inward-looking character of the text
- the persistent anti-Jewish statements

thinking positively about the 'sectarian' character of John
- the perspective of the minority
- the character of the political struggle open to a minority group: the usefulness of James Scott's Domination and the Arts of Resistance: Hidden Transcripts

'unless you are born again': the effect of John's gospel
- the experience of reading John is to challenge one to see things from the perspective of the Stranger from heaven and his followers
- John lacks argument: Jesus persists in offering enigmatic sayings to bewilder and lead to new ways of thinking and behaving

'changing sides'
- Nicodemus: the proper perspective on Jesus means leaving the elite and joining the minority and the outcasts
- the healings in John 5 & 9: the contrasting attitudes of those who are healed: the outsider understands (9.35f)

dialogue with Pilate
- turning the tables on the politically powerful
- Jewish elite asserts 'we have no king but Caesar', thereby turning the Passover statement of Israel's acknowledgement of God as the only lord on its head

5. Reports from the groups

The groups reported back in plenary as follows:

1. What came across as liberative texts in John
- Jn.9: Chronic and permanent illness - no-one's fault
- Jn 8: men were shamed into going away
- Martha, Mary, Woman of Samaria - liberating
- water into wine - liberating for Methodists
- Jn 3: breaking out of tradition with something new coming into the world
- you have to see the light before you get new opportunities
- liberative things are non-punitive
- more time needed to be engaged with text
- difficulty of being focused

2. The need for criteria

- the context in which one reads affects how one reads - it varies from day to day and moment to moment
- all texts may be liberative : it depends on the approach and how the texts are used
- because I am in the culture I am in, I cannot exclude its liberative potential in another culture
- one's own personal pilgrimage is important

3. Points from the process

- importance of discursive preamble ('had a natter')
- mums and toddlers not being accepted in Church (they had to pay)
- church and 'jumping through hoops' (e.g. ordination and the need to 'play the game')
- market stall holder
- passion for the people
- taking our background seriously
- power : where does it lie (status v. person)
- winners and losers - who was in the Jesus/Pilate situation in Jn. 18-19
- subversion - the act of the powerless person
- knowing who you are (Jesus knew who he was - his focus was elsewhere)
- focus elsewhere is a way of subverting the system
- 'we did refer to the gospel in making these connections'
- there was heat, anger and frustration coming through. We looked at how the church colluded with the system. It makes people powerless to express themselves. If you jump out of its little box, it's a threat. The Gospel of John reflects the way in which little people stand up and are counted.
- other points: ways of understanding; identify with power struggles; dealing with problems in text; seeing connections 'after chat'; Jn 9 - outcast at beginning and is so at end, but in a new way: how can monologue be used?

4. Specific Texts

Jn 18 - 19: the powerless one turns the tables on the one with power. When Nelson Mandela was in prison he managed to take charge of the situation.

What it means to be poor in spirit.

Jn. 8 - sexuality debate - woman was not singled out as the only sinner in that group. Jesus didn't appear to single out sexual sins as being particularly heinous.

18

Jn 4 - the woman found herself being led into areas of her life she didn't expect to see opened up.

Jn. 3 - transformation involves leaving behind inherited faith. Being born from above = knowing in the heart. Personal faith is 'owned faith'.

Loneliness - ministry needed among the lonely (e.g. elderly)

6. A Personal Report - (1) Ruth Weston

There now follows the report of the process of the discussion in one of the groups, by Ruth Sharples Weston.

What I (Ruth) brought to the group - a situation

I had convened the church's social awareness group and we had run some effective campaigns on fair trade and debt. I also did a lot of work as a Christian in the local community. Since I had put myself forward to be a candidate for ordained ministry the church had told me that I needed experience of their other committees (I already had plenty of experience of other churches' committees). Often on my own with a young family I had no extra time to offer. The result was that instead of being active and effective on one committee, I sit passively unable to do anything but attend the meetings of several church committees.

I expressed my frustration at having to jump through hoops which rendered me ineffective in terms of actual Christian action. Also, I felt that the work I did in the community was not valued as church work.

The Group Process

As we gathered together as a group of mostly women (although the selection had been arbitrary) - we started chatting, and as we did so stories and experiences came to light, anger and frustration were expressed. We found much in common and there was lot of "something like that happened to me" in the conversation.

When we got round to reading the Bible passage - John chapter 18 and 19 - we read it in the light of our previous conversation. Jesus, we saw, had been compelled to face perceptions and expectations of himself which he did not hold. He challenged the religious system of his time, and was perceived to be a threat, and was crucified for it. We found a Jesus who could sympathise with our frustrations at church attitudes to our kinds of outreach work, such as running Mums and Toddlers, or running a market stall.

We recognised and were frustrated by our own powerlessness: the system is too big and strong for us to openly and effectively challenge it. In our positions, we felt it was only possible to subvert it, to find ways of getting under or over or around the system. We must smile and say yes, and then quietly get on and do our own thing.

The question in my mind then, was how to survive the strain of being one thing and doing another, how to maintain a sense of integrity and a sense of perspective while jumping through hoops, to satisfy the church?

One member of the group answered that question for me in her reflections on John 18. I heard her say that Jesus was able to withstand the weight of expectations and perceptions thrust upon him, because his focus was way beyond these concerns. His goal was God and nothing else really mattered. So Jesus was not afraid of Pilot and his power, and Jesus did not share his concerns. Thus, when Pilate asked about his Kingship, Jesus could not answer the question directly because it was not a question that made sense to him: there was no answer to give. Throughout John's Gospel, this was the case - people asked Jesus questions at human level, but the focus of Jesus was way beyond these concerns and his answers reflected that perspective. Indeed his answers did not really answer the questions he was asked at all. The authorities ultimately had no power over him because he did not recognise it (e.g. Cf Jn 19:10-11).

So, the way we survive, the way we maintain our integrity and sense of perspective, I learned, is to constantly be aware that our goal is way beyond the here and now, in God. If our ultimate goal is God, jumping through hoops or not jumping through hoops is irrelevant, and no one can have power over us as they could not have power over Jesus. He was his own person in God, and so are we.

<u>What I took with me</u>
I no longer felt alone. I now had friends who shared by experience and frustrations. Also, with the Bible passage as a focus, we not only supported one another but learnt from one another and found ways of dealing with the situations which we faced. For instance I found a way of living with a situation I could not change by seeing that my focus lay beyond it, to God.

As someone, for whom the Bible has not been a living, relevant text for some years, it was liberating to discover a Jesus who could sympathise with our sufferings and who could offer us some ways of dealing with these situations.

In sum, the experience of this Bible group work was enormously positive. I came away feeling a new energy and enthusiasm, I felt I was on the right track and I knew what I was about. And some of the friendships begun in that group continue to this day.

7. A Personal Report - (2) Anne Rusbridge

Anne Rusbridge contributed the following in the week after the occasion:

It was good to meet you at UTU. I thoroughly enjoyed the whole event, and I have come away with a lot of very positive thoughts and ideas, and a lot of practical tools to use in personal study and in group situations. As promised, my thoughts on the discussion group on Wednesday morning.

Where I am coming from -
I have been frustrated for many years about the inconsistency between bible and church – what is read (and believed) in church often does not reflect in practice in church life. The way the bible is interpreted in church also has a bias in favour of the wealthy, middle class church and the area in which I live. Within the church there is considerable resistance to questions and enquiry. More recently I have become aware of an even greater inconsistency between those inside the church and those outside. They speak different languages. The church seems unwilling to even acknowledge this situation, let alone change it to accommodate others.

I brought to the group - a situation -
For five years I had a stall on a weekly market to earn enough money to study theology. I did this because I could not get any of my questions answered in church, BUT through the experience on the market, I met so many people who had a deep faith or belief in God, who prayed regularly, who were aware of the presence of God within their everyday lives – some who found bible passages helpful – but none of them found the church relevant, or helpful, and most actually found the church antagonistic, unloving and certainly uncomfortable. My initial response was to leave the church and serve God in the world. I am actually training for the ordained ministry, because I feel this is my calling, but I want to bring this experience into my ministry.

21

The group discussion -
Enabled me to make a link with the story of Nicodemus because here is a 'conversation' where both sides are speaking different languages. Awareness of this gave me a sense of home.

As other group members shared their stories, I saw that many people are facing/addressing the same issues – I am not alone – and that gave me confidence to continue to seek ways of changing the situation. This led to a discussion of other texts relating to power and powerlessness, to the need sometimes to be subversive in order to stand in solidarity with the oppressed.

What was liberating about the experience was that the text was allowed to speak on its own – addressing an immediate issue – throwing light on a situation – without having an enquiry into the meaning of the text and trying to justify what we should and should not believe. I think it was the immediacy of the link or connection between situation and texts that was liberating.

What I am taking with me -
Enthusiasm, encouragement, a feeling of solidarity.
A desire to allow the text to speak to a situation more often.
An intention to share this method of discovery with others, starting with the stories first and then making the link with the biblical text.

Reflecting on the experience
It was like a firework – a series of brightly coloured sparks exploding one after the other – when that finished, a realisation that in the text of John were many helpful passages which are our hope, encouragement, strength. Our help is in the bible, not the church; but then we can create a strategy based on the bible to equip us in the church situation.

7. Some Concluding Reflections

Chris Rowland writes:

Without a detailed evaluation from the twenty or so participants, it is not possible to get a complete assessment of the value of the morning's Bible study. From the comments made at the time there seemed to be not only an engagement with and commitment to the task but also an enjoyment of the opportunities which it opened up both to explore a variety of relevant issues and the texts of Scripture themselves. For me as a facilitator there was some satisfaction in the method. That is mixed with a recognition of the extent to which certain fears about the process determined the way in which the study was constructed. Nowhere is this more true than in the way in which, in the initial remarks, I inserted some reflections of my own about issues which John's gospel raised. The extent to which these governed the subsequent discussions may be judged from the feedback reports that are included. It does reflect a chronic problem that I have had to confront, but with little clear sense of resolution, namely, the expectations that a professorial presence at an occasion is set up either as an authority figure or as a target of reproach. Such dynamics have become so much part of the interpretative experience that they deserve some comment. Even on those occasions such as the one described in this article) where there may be a recognition and where, certainly in recent years, there has been a clear delineation of my role in advance, this has proved inadequate to deal with the expectations that 'the professor' will/ should be able to expound the true meaning of the text, its background, whether that be a political reading or not. The sense of disappointment when I have set up a process rather than given a presentation has been palpable. To a considerable extent I forestalled that sense of disappointment, or better, I indicated my unwillingness to deal again with the sense of disappointment by hoping to satisfy that anticipated disappointment by saying something about the way in which I would deal with what has been a problematic text for liberation exegesis.

With the rise of a more participative exegesis there are important questions to be raised about the role of the expert. Despite the demands that are put on me to tell people what the text means, I try to resist offering a neat solution, not least because I firmly believe that there is every possibility that those who participate in the Bible study will have insights open to them which will be every bit as profound as anything that I can offer, and frequently more so. The primary task is to enable that to happen. I look for ways in which participants in biblical interpretation can utilise or appropriate my expertise as a professor of Holy Scripture as well as the mutual support, insight and constraints of reading together in community. It is not at all clear how to employ a professional exegete. Frequently there is either a demand for the expert to pronounce or to expound on a subject and for him to function as problem-solver rather than facilitator.

A parallel situation is described by Gerald West in his recent book[9] in an account of his work with grassroots Bible study in South Africa. He describes the careful and subtle way in which he as an academic was part of the process of biblical interpretation. The primary thing he got people to do was to attend to the detail of the text and to check a tendency to wander from it. He describes his role as a facilitator as an enabler of forms of criticism which would, if asked, require him to provide resources on the kind of situation, community and society which produced the text. The familiar resources of modern academic biblical study were not used as a 'way in' to the text, however. Rather the Bible study started with the life interests of the participants. The task of biblical scholars is not to do the reading for ordinary readers, nor simply to accept uncritically their readings. Rather it is to read the Bible, as he puts it, **'with'** ordinary readers. In so doing one has to be as aware as one can be of one's own interests, and discern and engage with the power relations implicit in the reading process. Andrew Curtis' research in inner city Sydney has also demonstrated the way in which untrained readers can use and contribute to biblical interpretation from their experience [10].

There is a continuing need to provide those basic tools which are needed to 'allow the faculties to act'. Ancient Jewish and Christian interpreters contented themselves with offering exegetical guidelines as a way of enabling interpretation of the Scripture to take place rather than doing the job for people which most commentaries tend to do, suggesting to the reader how to go about making the connections and using the text as a gateway to God's ways for themselves. Nevertheless, as scholars like Erasmus and Tyndale realised, there is a constant need to enable biblical literacy by the provision of the tools to be provided for the exploration to take place. One of these is going to be the assessment of the various manuscripts of the Bible, the other is translation, a third is the provision of the circumstances in which text and experience can be explored, the testing of those explorations in the light of the gospel, a fourth is the careful reflection which helps challenge lazy, self-indulgent, or superficial reflection, and a fifth is the different understandings and misunderstandings down the centuries which can inform and guide contemporary readings; and finally there is the use of historical imagination to aid understanding and reflection on the text. We should pause over the use of the phrase 'careful' reflection in this context. Exegesis in the contemporary world has come to mean the close reading of the text. Nevertheless the analytical and critical may not be the best way of understanding the Bible. This point is well made by the following quotation:

> There are two ways of reading. The first is when one reads and puts oneself and one's mind in control of the text, trying to subject its meaning to one's own understanding and then comparing it with the understanding of others.
> The second is when one reads putting the text on a level above oneself, trying to bring one's mind into submission to its

meaning, and even setting up the text as judge over oneself, counting it as a higher criterion.

The first way is suitable for any book in the world, whether it be a world of science or of literature. The second is indispensable in reading the Bible.

The first way gives humans mastery over the world, which is their natural role. The second gives God mastery as the all-wise and all-powerful Creator.

But if we confuse the roles of these two methods, we stand to lose from them both. For if we read science and literature as we should the Gospel, we grow small in stature, our academic ability diminishes and our dignity among the rest of creation dwindles.

And if we read the Bible as we should science, we understand and feel God to be small, the divine being appears limited and His awesomeness fades. Thus we acquire a false sense of our own superiority over divine things, and this is the very same forbidden thing that Adam committed in the beginning.[11]

Down the centuries there have been two poles of exegesis: letter and spirit. Close reading of the text can be so preoccupied with the letter of the text, that its call to repentance, its offer of hop can be missed. If we concentrated on close reading only, we would risk missing the importance that Paul (among others) places on the spirit which gives life rather than the letter which kills. Fear of the 'spiritual exegesis' of the radicals since the Reformation should not diminish the central role it most play in the exegesis of Scripture. When I read the gospels in the contemporary academy I am surrounded by a plethora of interpretative approaches, but I approach the text as a problem. Scripture is treated as a problem which the 'enlightened' interpreter can solve. The emphasis in criticism is on analysis and not enough on silence, contemplation and imagination. If I read the Bible, say, as part of the Ignatian Exercises, I put myself in a very different relationship to the text: of hearer, of subject, even of suppliant. The attitude of mind is very different. The challenge, in this case is to oneself in the first instance rather than to the Scriptures. Of course, modern readers, however much they are committed to the 'receptionist' approach, will find themselves at times perplexed and resistant to Scripture. They will engage in analysis and explanation, puzzling over the way it overlaps, or not, s the case may be, with their contemporary experience of life. The kind of attitude I have in mind is that which Coleridge wrote about in his words: 'in the Bible there is more that finds me than have experienced in all other books put together'. Coleridge feared both those who elevated the Bible and its details as much as those who dissected the text of Scripture and thereby killed its spirit. The bibliolaters and the textual analysts have this in common that they do not allow themselves to be in that passive mode, to allow the Bible to, (to quote William Blake's words) 'rouze the faculties to act'. Now that will not always work. Many times we shall find ourselves in the position of not engaging with the text. Many people have said to me when I have told them that I am interested in the Apocalypse that they found the book barbarous and off-putting and that it should not form part of a Christian canon. There are two responses. First of all, what is it about us in our time and place that we cannot engage with the book? Have we a view of Christianity which is so safe and cosy that we cannot see the way in which the gospel, with all its stories and metaphors, hold up a mirror to our world and reflects a picture of injustice and disorder where we only see comfort and order. But, secondly, is God calling us to a task of obedient receptivity in which we learn to find images and stories which capture what the Spirit says to the churches much as John found himself using images which doubtless were part of the mental furniture of his day? That was what Blake was doing in his illuminated books. The mistake would be to suppose that task is finished and all we have to do is to interpret what is past. What we need to do is to go on finding, or better allowing ourselves to be receptive to God showing us, ever-new ways of communicating the challenge and comfort of the gospel.

---

[1] D. Rensberger, Overcoming the World. London: SPCK, 1988.

[2] J. Ashton, Studying John: Approaches to the Fourth Gospel. Oxford, OUP, 1994 p. 206f

[3] This is one of the points made by Nicholas Lash in his essay 'What Might Martyrdom Mean ?" in his collection Theology on the Way to Emmaus. London, SCM, 1986.

[4] C. Mesters, 'The Use of the Bible in Christian Communities of the Common People' in ed. Norman Gottwald, The Bible and Liberation. New York: Orbis, 1983 and C. Mesters, Defenseless Flower. Orbis, 1989; G. West, Biblical Hermeneutics of Liberation. Cluster Publications. Pietermaritzburg, 1991.

[5] G. West, The Academy of the Poor : Towards a Dialogical Reading of the Bible. Sheffield : Sheffield Academic Press, 1999.

[6] On the similarities see the forthcoming collection edited by Andrew Bradstock and Christopher Rowland, Radical Christian Writings: A Reader. Oxford: Blackwells, 2001.

[7] G. West, The Academy of the Poor : Towards a Dialogical Reading of the Bible. Sheffield : Sheffield Academic Press, 1999.

[8] See pp. 44-51 of the present volume.

[9] G. West, The Academy of the Poor : Towards a Dialogical Reading of the Bible. Sheffield : Sheffield Academic Press, 1999.

[10] Andrew Curtis, Re-reading the Gospel of Luke Today : From a First Century Urban Writing Site to a Twentieth Century Urban Reading Site. Open University Diss., 1998.

[11] Words of Abba Matta El-Meskeen, founder of the Monastery of St Macarius, Wadi El-Natrun, Egypt and printed in their monthly journal St Mark, November 1981.

Jenny Richardson

YOU CAN KEEP YOUR HAT ON!

When I was interviewed for local radio, the presenter told me "I enjoyed the film "The Full Monty", but I must admit I didn't think it had potential as a basis for Bible studies". A couple of weeks later I heard that the staff in an academic institution had laughed scornfully at the suggestion that it be used in one of their Bible studies. Their reaction, "You can't possibly do real Bible study based on a film like that" implied that it was not possible to relate the Bible and the experiences of a group of unemployed men in Sheffield.

These responses indicate the gulf that exists between attempts to connect the Bible and life in the UK's inner city and housing estate areas, and more conventional ways of approaching Bible study. Fortunately, other responses have been more positive, confirming that the raw material of life can be placed alongside Bible stories, for meaningful dialogue and illumination of both, giving opportunity for urban people to make their own sense of their stories in the light of the Bible, and vice versa.

I'm going to focus on a Bible pack based on the Full Monty video, to outline the method used by Unlock, formerly the Evangelical Urban Training Project (EUTP), in its approaches to the Bible. EUTP began in the early 1970s from a concern that much training and education (and theology) within church structures was from the perspective of those who have been successful within the educational and other systems of this country.

Janet Rourke, a Church Army worker in Liverpool, and at that time linked with EUTP, was aware of the need to affirm those who had been rejected by most forms of church education, and developed what she termed "Simple Bible Studies". Some of these are still in use, effectively, and they have been a foundation for further development. Janet wrote,

> I have always worked with urban people, but my Christian experience has taken me away from my own working class roots. I have been moulded into a middle class person. In East London I hadn't really been part of the community and when I went to Huyton (Merseyside) I had to look again at my roots. What had the church done to me? How much of my ideas about the Gospel were preconceived? It was a great relief when I found that I could stop having to go to the top of a view in the Lake District and say, "Oh! Isn't God wonderful." I could experience God in my own urban scene. The Bible speaks to everyday life and I needed to find some way of relating it to the small groups I am working with. These Bible studies have been used by a group of 7 people. I doubt whether many of them read anything more than a newspaper. They are not book people. I don't think there's a book in X's house.[1]

The Bible studies ask a few questions along the lines of "Have you ever ....?", giving people an opportunity to share some of their own experiences in a story form, and then the group share a related Bible story - one person can read this to the rest of the group, or some passages are set out as a dramatic reading.

Traditional Bible study begins with analysis of the text, moving on to deduct general principles. This approach provides a logical framework, and the person stores the information (in his/her mind, in note form, or on disc) for use when needed. It requires a way of thinking and communicating which is based on linear methods of learning, linked with activity of the left side of the brain. I would suggest that this thinking style is that encouraged by the dominant culture in modernity, and deviations from it have in many cases been regarded as less than ideal. "Deviants" have included those from working class cultures, and those whose personality prefers artistic expression rather than logic. The move towards post modern culture is giving validity to a wider variety of thinking patterns, and a growing number of people are finding linear learning methods are inappropriate. My experience leads me to believe that these styles have never been appropriate in the inner city and housing estate areas of the UK.

Paulo Freire[2] compares banking and teamwork methods of education; the former assumes that learners are empty vessels to be filled; the latter encourages dialogue between learners and teachers, with the expectation that all learn and all teach. Traditional Bible study assumes that the group of learners need to be taught the truth of the Christian faith and the Bible by

28

those who whose know more - usually those who have been through formal theological training - thus following the banking method of teaching and learning. Walter Wink notices the irrelevance of this theological expertise: "Like the wealthy cargo of the merchant ships in Revelation 18, much biblical scholarship has become "... a luxury good, largely unrelated to the struggles of real people for liberation, dignity or a reason to live."[3] These analytical Bible study methods are alien to many whose preference is to watch TV, read tabloids and meet friends in the pub and bingo hall, rather than read books and follow more formal educational routes. In urban areas, this has always been an issue; it is becoming relevant to more of the church, as middle class and formally educated young people are becoming less inclined to read books, and are preferring to communicate via other means.

A housegroup from an inner city parish, attempting to use a Bible study following a banking format, told me recently, "We sometimes don't get onto the proper study - we just stop with the icebreaker questions" - which on closer inspection are those that encourage the telling of personal experiences, rather than an exploration of the text. A vicar told me of his experience as he moved from a renowned academic establishment to life in the inner city. He'd seen a road accident on the way to a church meeting, and in his shaken state, recounted the incident to a small group of the local people. He had quite expected to find the group asking him questions about his story, to understand more, and indicate their careful listening. Instead, someone told him of an accident he had seen a few years earlier - he showed his care and concern by sharing another story, rather than analysing the one first offered. It seems that this is a key in bringing the Bible alongside those who prefer to communicate through story. The Bible story, from another time and another culture, can stand alongside with the day to day struggles of people in urban UK, showing solidarity.

These two examples indicate the need for an approach to the Bible based on sharing stories of life. Using this insight, Unlock's method is based on a spiral:[4]

Unlocking real life stories of urban people
Revealing Good News of the Down to Earth Christ
Releasing life changing skills and confidence

2. Unlocking Real Life Stories of Urban People

Freire advocated an educational style based on teamwork learning[5], and the process of conscientisation for all, as they discovered together more understanding of their situation. He listened carefully, teasing out key issues for a community, and presenting people with the issue in a different context (for example, through a visit to a similar situation, a photograph or a picture). This he termed a "code", which is a concrete representation of a familiar problem. A code raises questions and shows the problem; it does not provide solutions. Once people saw that the situation was not good, Freire asked, "Does it happen round here?" and people were able to express how they felt about a situation, with motivation to act for change based on strong feelings.

Watching the film the Full Monty in Sheffield was a privilege. In many ways, it crystallised aspects of life in the inner city part of Sheffield where I live - the frustration and resignation about unemployment; the sense of solidarity that people exhibit - and the zany humour! I was not surprised that it was a talking point for those I met as I went around Sheffield. What surprised me more was the reaction of those in other inner city areas. It seemed to draw discussion about life from those I met as I travelled around the housing estate areas of several cities, as part of my national role with Unlock. I realised that the film was "unlocking" stories of people' life experiences in very natural ways, and was in many ways acting as a code; a representation of life as we know it, enabling people to talk about what's going on in the film and then quite naturally moving to their own stories. Key themes for story telling emerged quickly, and recognising Biblical resonance was straightforward. In some ways the production of an Unlock pack, "Go For It" based on "The Full Monty" was a bit like a rerun of the film - could we, a small organisation, actually make this happen, against the odds? We even experienced the humour! Communication over copyright for the film was hampered, we realised, by accidentally sending the first letter to the film company on 1st April!! It was only when we sent a second letter with a different date that they treated it anything like seriously!!! The printing firm had problems, and were reported to be singing "We believe in miracles" as they wrestled with machinery!

So, clips from the video are used as codes, and people are asked to share their own experiences. For example, a clip early on in the video shows Lomper trying to commit suicide and Gaz and Dave preventing this happening. Their reflection together sitting on the bank overlooking Sheffield leads them to consider other methods of suicide (like bungey jumping, but without the bungey bit!) and finally it's proposed that Lomper stands in the middle of the road and gets a mate to run into him right fast. His mournful response is that he has no mates - and Dave responds "Don't tell us we're not your mates ... I'd run into you soon as look at you." Lomper is clearly moved by this declaration of friendship from Dave and Gaz. This clip, with questions like "Who are your mates" and "What makes a good mate?" have then drawn out

30

considerable sharing. Local groups that meet regularly have affirmed their own friendship; people have shared stories of times when life has been rough and particular people have stood by them; regular church goers have recognised that their real friendships are in the pub not the congregation, and I have heard church ministers admit that they have no real friends. The sharing of stories helps a group strengthen its relationships, and it is a natural progression for a Bible story to be put alongside the other stories.

3. Revealing Good News of the Down to Earth Christ

The Bible passage that we chose to use next to the stories about "mates" is Acts 2 v43-47 - a picture of life in the early church, where people "continue together in close fellowship." Discussions have experienced a richness brought to the text from the stories of mates in ordinary life - and the word "fellowship" is no longer immediately tarnished with images of cups of tea and digestive biscuits!

At a consultation about the Bible in pastoral practice[6], it was clear that an ongoing debate is around the question of whether we sit alongside the Bible as Christians, or under its authority. The latter brings with it the major problem of how we decide which particular parts to sit under, and which parts we will choose to ignore. The method of using the Bible in the example I am describing is an attempt to place the Bible story alongside the real life experiences of those engaged in the study - in solidarity with them.

Another issue regarding using the Bible in this context is the presentation of the Bible, for those who do not readily choose to engage with text. The Tabloid Bible[7] has succeeded in producing an authentic tabloid presentation of each page. However, it is a paraphrase, rather than Biblical text, and is bound into a book so that it can't be used in "bite sized chunks". Other magazine formats for the publication of a gospel are again a step in the right direction, but their style is reminiscent of a glossy magazine. They are still providing a reader with far more text than they would normally encounter, and the reading age of the Good News Bible is higher than the reading age for the Sun newspaper. Other alternatives include audio-visual media. The most comprehensive audio cassette version of the Bible that I am aware of comes with "strings attached" - it is only available through church leaders, requiring a commitment to an entire listening plan determined by the producers. A recent film, "The Miracle Maker" has been one example, among others, of a visual story based presentation of the life of Jesus, with a commitment to an authentic representation of the culture of the historical Jesus.

31

4. Releasing Life Changing Skills and Confidence

The last stage in the process is for those who've shared their stories and reflected on the Bible, to look at what are the next steps of action for themselves as a group, or as individuals, with implications for their neighbours.

Reactions from those who've used the example given have been varied. One church decided to create opportunities to eat meals together informally. A group of students at a Bible college realised that they tended to just sit with their own friends at meal times, and made a commitment to each other to sit with those they didn't know so well on a more regular basis. A small group meeting on a housing estate recognised the quality of their support and friendship with each other, when they felt that there wasn't much going for them as a church in what they and others saw as a rough area. I am aware of individuals who have made private pacts with themselves to appreciate more those who stand by them, and to value friendship for its own sake.

5. Concerns and Criticisms

A valid criticism of this method is that peoples' stories are complex, and cannot fit neatly into a theme to attach to a Bible story. The packs provide an introduction to this method, and those who are experienced at enabling a group to tell their stories, brainstorm resonating Bible passages, and identify those texts they wish to explore further don't need the packs! It would be Unlock's dream to develop this ability in all those who encourage groups to engage with the Bible!

An issue for some using Unlock materials has been around the question of which should come first, the Bible or experience. Groups that have been used to more traditional methods have struggled with bringing the Bible in second - feeling that they are not sure what they should be talking about at the beginning, because they don't know the right answer. Once a group gives itself permission to begin with their experiences, the result can be liberating. A "ladies fellowship" group in suburbia used the pack, and discovered that instead of spending the evening analysing a text, and trying to work out what it meant, they were delighted to find: "we talked to each other"!!

I visited a church with established neighbourhood groups where a group of people regularly meet together to share their own news and news of the neighbourhood, and reflect together on the Bible. At the meeting I attended, with the vicar, they said to him "You should have been here last week. We were struggling with the passage. We needed you to sort it out for us". In fact, the week before, they had reached some reflections themselves with great insight, and yet were not confident that they had found the right answer. This is a difficult role for clergy and those with Bible training. They may make every effort to sit alongside a group, and serve them, but they are working within a tradition where church members have learned to defer to those with "spiritual authority" as a result of their Biblical knowledge or their position within the church. By way of contrast, another group of local people I visited on a housing estate, who were engaged in "doing theology" realised that the most valuable contribution made by their minister was not his Biblical expertise ("We could have used a concordance") but the use of his large living room, as a space for the group to meet!

Those who have trained in theology and Biblical studies question whether there is a role for them in this process. It seems that those who prefer the more traditional approaches to Biblical education see their role in two parts: one is an understanding of the text itself, and its background and the other is an application of the text to the context.

The first part of their role is a valuable contribution to a group who are looking at the Bible for themselves. Cardenal, sharing the Bible exploration with a group of poor farmers and fishermen in Nicaragua,[8] clearly offers his Bible knowledge to the group who are dialoguing together around the Bible text. However, the important aspect of this is that the Biblical background material is at the service of the group, rather than controlling it.

The second part of the role is taken up by the group who define their own context, and use the background material to make their own connections. Often, the social situation of the person who has the Bible knowledge is different from that of the group studying, and it is the group themselves who can make the relevant links.

Thinking back to the incredulous comments about linking the Full Monty and the Bible, detailed at the beginning, my reflection is that if we can't look at the Bible in relation to the fictional lives in the film, and their representation of life in the part of inner city Sheffield which is my home, then we have to assume that the Bible has no relevance for the transformation of that part of the world that we care about. Thankfully, my experiences prove this viewpoint to be wrong - but it's indicative of the chasm that exists between theology that is "trickled down" to us from those with educational power, and theology that emerges from our real lives as we encounter God where we are.

[1] Experience the Bible, page 22. "Experience the Bible", the up to date version of Simple Bible studies, is available from Unlock.

[2] Paulo Freire, Pedagogy of the Oppressed. Penguin, 1972 pp. 45ff.

[3] Walter Wink, Transforming Bible Study. Abingdon Press, 1980 pp. 98, 99.

[4] Unlock's method is based on a theological spiral, documented in Laurie Green, Let's Do Theology. Mowbray, 1990 p.42.

[5] Paulo Freire, Pedagogy of the Oppressed. Penguin, 1972 pp. 45ff, 81ff.

[6] Consultation about the Bible in Pastoral practice: Cardiff University and the Open Book project of the Bible Society; June 2000.

[7] Nick Page, The Scroll: The Tabloid Bible. HarperCollins, 1998

[8] Ernesto Cardenal, Love in Practice: The Gospel in Solentiname. Search Press Ltd, 1977.

Janet Lees
REMEMBERING THE BIBLE IN WORSHIP

Ever tried a bible study without a bible?

Ever wondered how to join in if you can't read the bible?

As a speech therapist I'm used to working with people who find using written material difficult, and those who have many other kinds of communication problems. This has lead to the development of ways of using remembered versions of the bible, rather than using written versions all of the time. Since August 1998 we have been using remembered versions of the Bible in worship in some of the member churches of the Sheffield Inner City Ecumenical Mission. Here a group of people from those churches introduce themselves and that method.

1. Three Churches' Experience

'We are an ecumenical group of small churches in the north of Sheffield at the heart of deprivation, poverty and unemployment, with a wide diversity of races and cultures in our area. The churches came together in most cases because the alternative was closure. Struggle is what we are used to as churches and communities.

We've been using remembered texts for about 2 years at the time of writing this. They have been used in work with people with communication difficulties who could not use the Bible in a written form. Our diverse congregations and community work experiences suggested we too could benefit from trying to use the Bible in this way. After all, communication difficulties are common in churches !! Here are some of the advantages and disadvantages we've found of using remembered versions of Bible stories in worship and study groups:

Advantages	Disadvantages
people participate	can't remember if you've never heard it before
it is interesting and lively, makes you think	may feel threatening if 'put on the spot'
can be surprised by how much we remember	stories can get mixed up in the remembering

We have also found there are some things that help us to remember
- sharing what we remember in a small group,
- a story which has repetititve bits which gradually we can join in,
- preparing in advance or working on it more than once,
- an informal setting
- clues from picture Bibles, films, musicals, plays, a cartoon, etc.,
- providing an outline of the story to fill in the details.

If you decide to try this yourselves don't worry that people will remember the wrong thing, or get it wrong in some way. We all remember things differently and the way memories are stored in our brains will differ. One person's version of a remembered text is likely to be different from anothers, but that doesn't make it wrong. Where people draw in parts of other episodes it can be helpful to explore why thy remember these things together. The process is trying to give people confidence to use the Bible as they have remembered it. Therefore try to encourage rather than discourage participants. It might also help them to understand other things about the Bible like

- the way the gospels were put together relied heavily on memory
- there were probably lots of different versions around in the early days.

We realise that some groups will hate using remembered texts. In our largely literate society the printed Bible has become indispensable for some groups, and they will find it very difficult or impossible to put it away. Don't assume that your group will be like this, but you may need to be ready to make allowances; some people like the back up of the written text somewhere (you can always read a written version aloud after the shared remembering if you prefer). If you want to use these methods then the leadership team needs to have an idea who might be good at starting the group off on remembering episodes from Jesus life story,

- prepare in advance some of the material which will give people clues about these,
- be gentle and take sufficient time for the task (both preparation and during worship).

It can take some time to reconstruct a remembered text with a group and may include lots of silences. Try not to rush them - silence is not a waste of time.

We know it is a huge generalisation to say that 'there is a Bible in everyone' but we hope you will try to discover something about the ones the group members have in them. We have noticed that
- being comfortable in the group rather than knowing lots about the Bible makes for success in this process
- children, who may not have heard as much of the Bible before as some older members, often participate more readily because story telling is something they do more often in other ways,
- some of the members who say little at times may have a lot more to contribute to the remembering process,
- the whole thing can be done nonverbally, by mime or through drawings, if many of the group members are nonverbal.

We hope you enjoy using remembered texts."

Members of Pitsmoor Methodist Church, St James URC and Shiregreen URC, in the Sheffield Inner City Ecumenical Mission.

2. Methods of Making a Remembered Text

So how is it done? Here are some ways of making a remembered text with a group. You may use them with groups of different sizes (they have been used with groups from 2-200 people), although if the whole group is very large then some small group work initially is probably helpful. Small group work does not need to be formal but may just mean talking to the few people sitting next to you.

1. Flip chart outline method.
On a flip chart put the main outline of the story in about half a dozen headings. These need to represent the beginning, middle and end of the story. Then invite the group to fill in each section. For example, three headings for 'Jesus heals a blind person' might be A blind person heard Jesus was approaching

37

Jesus healed the blind person

The group moved on somewhere else.

The group can then be invited to fill in the story as they remember it from the prompts.

2. Finish off the sentence method.

Have a version of the story written out on cards in single sentences which are left unfinished. Present the sentences in order and invite the group to finish off each sentence as they think appropriate. This method is helpful if you fear no one will remember anything. For the same story about the blind person some of these might be

A blind person was...................

Jesus asked the blind person....................

The blind person replied.....................

3. Animated method.

Have some small toys, cut outs or puppets to represent the characters of the story and invite some members of the group to move these around as directed by other members of the group. In small groups you might want to suggest that one group thinks about the activities of one character, whilst another group does another character, etc.

4. Rehearsed method.

Ask people to look at the story in advance of the week you want to use it and come ready to retell it to each other. This is a good method for the group that thinks it can't do this, or won't like doing it, but don't mind doing some homework.

5. Picture method or 'Rolf Harris method'.

Use a picture Bible, some cartoons or a large painting illustrating the main events of the story, or even a reproduction of a well known painting representing the events, as a trigger to help people remember.

Ruth Maxey of Weoley Castle URC tried this method:

'I did a large cartoon on a backcloth of a scene from the Wedding at Cana. I put some empty speech bubbles on the cartoon and I inivited people to come up and fill them in with what they thought people might have said. There were some really good ideas which allowed people to explore what the story was really about'.

If people were not mobile enough to come up and join in, either find a way to bring the picture to them or ask people to work in groups where groups members share a range of mobility.

6. Storyteller method.

This is for the group who remember nothing and who hate joining in. Find one or two people from the group who are willing to tell the story in their own words, either to small groups or the whole group. They might want to practise the story first. This can be followed by getting the group/s to retell what they have heard to each other.

7. Go for it method.

Just go for it and see what happens. Invite people in small or large groups to discuss what they remember of the story. After they have done this one person can collect up their responses episode by episode, checking with other groups/people to see what level of agreement is reached. The whole agreed version can be retold at the end. This is the riskiest method and usually takes the longest.

Remember that the idea is to produce something you have remembered together, not a word for word version of any particular written translation but something that has come from the groups response to how the story is recalled by them all. It may be chaotic but don't be afraid of that. It can be fun!
You may want to finish you remembered text with the response:

'This is to us the Gospel of Christ.'

'Praise to Christ our Lord.'

3. Some Trouble-Shooting Examples

Here's some trouble shooting examples from real life to encourage you to have a go despite the difficulties you think you might encounter.

'I don't remember anything'.
There's always someone who says this. It may be true. You must hear what is said but there's no need to make a big thing of it or stop the process if one or two or even most people say this. Firstly they may be bluffing. Secondly this might be code for 'I don't do this sort of thing in church'. You have to decide whether or not you are still going to 'go for it'. A good antedote is to say 'Well what do you think happened first?' It is unlikely they can't think of something which will begin the process. For example:

JAL: We are going to remember the story of Jesus healing a blind person.

HLW (actually my 7 year old daughter): I don't remember that one.

JAL: Well what do you think happened first.

HLW: There was a blind person.

JAL: Right, and what was happening? What did blind people do in those days?

HLW: Nothing? The blind person was sitting by the road doing nothing.

JAL: OK, so what happened next.

HLW: Jesus came by.

JAL: And then....

'I can't remember if it was Martha or Mary'

It is not unusual for people to get muddled about the names of those taking part in gospel stories. What you have to decide is how important this is and how to resolve any resulting differences of opinion. The best thing to do is encourage a discussion. The more they talk it out the more people will grapple with the issues themselves. It is unlikely you will have to arbitrate. The group will, given time, come up with its own solution.

'Well Jesus went round to the home of Andrew's Mother-in-Law'

This one is rather more obviously apocryphal (in case you're unsure Jesus is said to have visited Simon's mother-in-law in three of the gospels). Again, it depends on the point being made as to what you might do. Once the group gets the hang of the process they are more likely to deal with differences like this creatively. After all, we don't know if Andrew had a mother-in-law (socially speaking quite likely) or if Jesus went to see her (again not impossible). All we can say is the gospel writers didn't mention it. All these are good opportunities to discuss how the written gospels were assembled and what authority they have for us today. See Andrew's mother-in-law as an opportunity rather than a threat.

We can't do this, we've got pews'

Oh, yes you can! It's been done loads of times. Take time to explain what is going to happen and encourage people to work where they are with those they are sitting nearby. Usually habitual seating patterns mean that they have seen these people before and that shouldn't be too threatening. Don't expect too much at once. The first time may take longer and people may be unsure. Encourage them and keep at it. Of course there may be people who are sitting next to no one at all. Whilst this may be further indication that church furniture needs discussing at the next church meeting, for the purposes of this exercise it is also fine to invite people to remember the story for themselves, by themselves. OK, so you can't check to see if they are doing it, but don't assume they aren't.

4. Remembering the Last Supper

Using remembered versions of the Bible has also influenced the way we use the Bible at other times in worship. The Maundy Thursday evening service for 2000 at Shiregreen URC included a good example of this in the form of a short drama about the Last Supper.

In this drama are a number of specific features relevant to the way we use the Bible together:
- it includes all ages together; the drama had participants from 9 years of age upwards,
- it builds on the common experiences we share; in this case it is based around our experiences of running a community project and the meetings that are involved in this,
- it includes bits of the Bible we have remembered and worked with during the year; references to feeding the 5,000, healing Peter's mother in law, visiting Martha and Mary, and the Holy Week narrative itself are amongst these,
- it includes some of the background to studying the Bible which we have discussed, for example its gender bias,
- it shares features with common culture, in this case the television 'sitcom' genre, which is familiar to us all.

The Last Supper

Cast: Jesus (J), Martha (M), Peter (P), Judas, Thomas, at least 4 speaking disciples (D1-4) and one unspeaking Mary.

D1   Is this the meeting of the Disciples of Jesus Executive Committee ?

D2   Yes it is and you're late

D1   I'm sorry, it's my first meeting

D2   It'll be your last if you don't buck up.

J   Right, well let's get this show on the road. Appiontment of officers for this meeting. Peter, you take the minutes, Martha, you make the tea. Second item, minutes of the last meeting, held at Martha's house, any comments?

M   Yes, I don't see a record here of what I actually said. Peter seems to have left it out. I said 'You are the Christ the Messiah', but he hasn't put that.

41

J   Yes, Peter why did you leave that out.

P *(mumbling)* Women, I knew we shouldn't have had any on this committee *(corrects paper)*.

D3   I see Mary's here again.   Why does she come, she never says anything?

D4   I know what you mean. You'd have thought she'd have stayed away after the scene she made at that meeting at Simon's house when she poured all that perfume over the Chair.

J   All right you two, that will do. If some of the verbal people here thought as much about what they said as Mary thinks about what she doesn't say we'd get along a lot better. Item Three, a report from the catering subcommittee. Peter, wasn't your mother in law going to present that. She doesn't seem to be here.

P   Well she's got a headache so she's stayed at home. *(mumbles)* Best place for her if you ask me.

J   Martha are you going to present that item then ?

M   Yes, I could do if you like. We just wanted to say, it's getting a bit difficult on the catering side when we don't know how many are going to turn up. I know you managed with those couple of fish and out of date bread cakes that time, but with a bit more organisation we could do a nice spread.

J   Martha, Martha you are troubled by many things. How many times do I have to explain it to you all? Look, it's simple *(takes bread cake)* this is my body broken for you *[pause]*- got it? Now can we crack on, I've got an appointment in the Garden of Gethsemane in an hour.

P   Could we take the financial report from Judas before he has to go ? *(mumurs of agreement from others)*.

Judas   Well, there's not much to say. We're about 30 pieces of silver down on the month's end balance but I hope to have sorted that out by the end of the evening.

J   Yes, I know you have to leave early Judas. Could you try to leave quietly please. Hope to catch you later. Now where had we got to? *(Judas leaves)*

M   I think that brings us to the date of the next meeting. That should be Joseph's house on Sunday evening I think.

J   Well, I'll not be there. In fact *(takes cup)* - I'll not drink of the fruit of the vine again until I drink it in my Father's kingdom.

P   Not be there? But what do you mean? You're always there. You said, where two or three are gathered together you'd always be

	there. We can't have a meeting without you *(murmurs of agreement)*.
J	Yes, well I was going to say something about that Peter. Do you ever think we might be getting a bit bogged down with meetings?
D1	Bogged down ?
D2	With meetings ?
All	We don't know what you mean.
J	I see. Well, perhaps I could arrive a bit late.
Thom	A bit late! But you know we always lock the door when the meeting starts so no one can interupt us. So if you're going to turn up late, how will we recognise you ?
All	*(turn towards Jesus)* Yes, how will we recognise you ?

The drama proved to be a successful way of delivering the Maundy Thursday story to this mixed age congregation. As one participant said afterwards: 'I never understood what it was about before'. Using remembered texts we had worked with together, and basing the reflection on common shared experience, provided a framework in which we could all relate to the story and understand it's relevance to our situation 2000 year on. Try it - you might like it!

Timothy Gorringe

BIBLE AND SUBVERSION

1. Is Scripture Subversive?

'The Devil can cite Scripture to his purpose'. To any claim that Scripture is, in and of itself subversive, the objector can point to the many reactionary or evil purposes it has been used to support. We know that Scripture was used by the 'double Reformed' church in South Africa to justify apartheid. Further back it was used to justify the persecution of so-called 'heretics', Jews, Protestants by Catholics and Catholics by Protestants. Feminist theologians have a strong case in arguing that Scripture emanates from a patriarchal culture and cannot but propagate one. Charles Raven believed that the Old Testament was irredeemably violent, and wanted to exclude it from the Christian canon on those grounds. So we have the objection which was raised in the sixteenth century that Scripture is a 'wax nose which any rogue can mould to his face'. Luther and Calvin's response was to insist on 'the plain sense of scripture' but this recourse is not available to us. Not that the awareness that there is no innocent reading is new to us: the problem of interpretation is an ancient one. For Philo and Origen the need to distinguish between different senses, in which the literal sense was the lowest form, may have been occasioned by what was felt to be the crudity of the Scriptural narratives when set alongside Plato or other Greek philosophers. In its attempt to counter medieval theology the Reformation went back to the literal sense, but the disagreements of more than a century begot another intensive round of reflection on the problem of interpretation, of the question of what might constitute 'objectivity' when there is no view from nowhere.

The academic debate has made some progress, but with regard to the church we see the problems we still have both in the reactionary use of scripture as in the notorious 'Sermon on the Mound', or for that matter in Vatican

Instructions on Liberation Theology, and in the prohibition of the teaching of evolution as 'counter to scripture' in Bible belt America.

If Christians cannot agree on what exactly constitutes the heart of Scripture, how can we claim that it is subversive? Our star witness for the case that it is, of course, is Nietzsche. For all its since, liberal Protestantism must have been getting something right for Nietzsche to object as strongly as he did to the gospel. I quote a famous passage from *The Anti Christ* which bears directly on the project of liberation theology.

> That, as an 'immortal soul', everybody is equal to everybody else, that in the totality of beings the 'salvation' of every single one is permitted to claim to be of everlasting moment, that little bigots and three-quarters of madmen are permitted to imagine that for their sakes the laws of nature are continually being broken - such a raising of every sort of egoism to infinity, to impudence, cannot be branded with sufficient contempt ... The poison of the doctrine 'equal rights for all' this has been more thoroughly sowed by Christianity than by anything else; from the most secret recesses of base instincts, Christianity than by anything else; from the most secret recesses of base instincts, Christianity has waged war to the death gainst every feeling of reverence of reverence and distance between man and man ... it has forged out of the *ressentiment* of the masses its chief weapon against us, against everything noble, joyful, high spirited on earth, against our happiness on earth ... 'Immortality' granted to every Peter and Paul has been the greatest and most malicious outrage on noble mankind ever committed. And let us not underestimate the fatality that has crept out of Christianity even into politics! No one any longer possesses today the courage to claim special privileges or the right to rule, the courage to feel a sense of reverence towards himself and towards his equals - the courage for a pathos of distance ... Our politics is morbid from this lack of courage.[1]

Nietzsche felt that Christianity preached a 'slave morality', that it opposed a healthy, joyous, and strong affirmation of life with a morbid concentration on suffering. Hence it was necessary to oppose Dionysus to the Crucified. It has to be granted, of course, that in the Lutheran tradition Nietszche knew at first hand (he was a child of the manse) there was much which was morbid, but it seems to me that he goes beyond this to essentials. He has seen *both* that there is a priority to the poor in the gospel, *and* that this has political consequences. And he does not like it. Here he is much more clear sighted than Christian advocates of the rule of the strong, all those right wing cardinals who opposed and still oppose, liberation theology, all those who sought to silence Leonardo Boff, all those, in Britain, who believe that the gospel is instantiated in managerial capitalism. For Nietzsche the gospel was *subversive* of a strong political order. This makes the point that the term 'subversion' relates to the undermining of some dominant set of values or societal structures. It can be good or bad, healthy or unhealthy. In asking whether the gospel is subversive we need to outline those dominant values which are undercut, and I do that in relation to Walter Wink's account of the 'delusional assumptions' of our society and Susan George's chilling account of what is needed to preserve capitalism in the twenty first century, *The Lugano Report.*

2. "Delusional Assumption"

Wink highlights sixteen 'delusional assumptions'. Amongst them are these: Structures of domination are required to keep anarchy at bay; men are better equipped to dominate than women, and some races than other races; violence is redemptive; ruling or managing is the most important social function; money is the most important value; property is sacred; institutions are more important than people.[2] From Susan George's 'Report', a fiction but based on a careful analysis of the statements of corporations and institutions like the World Bank and the World Trade Organisation we can add the following: self-interest is what motivates people; the free market is an instantiation of divine providence; social inequality is essential to human flourishing; religions must stick to their proper concern and not interfere in polities.[3]

Given that there are card carrying Christians who believe all of these propositions, it cannot be simply taken for granted that Scripture subverts them. Rather, we are in the position of those Christian anti-apartheid campaigners in South Africa who had to argue head to head with their fellow Christians who supported apartheid on what constitutes the true sense of Scripture. Let us take them in order:

Structures of domination are needed to keep anarchy at bay

It is an ancient theme amongst Christians, going back at least to Augustine's *City of God,* that strong government is needed to curb violent propensities of human sin. If we needed any convincing, need we look any *further than the* history of the twentieth century? The crucial issue, however, is as to the nature of the structures of authority. An unarmed police force, democratically funded, and democratically accountable, is one thing. Hitler's *Sturmabteilung,* Pinochet's troops, the South African police who murdered Steve Biko are quite another. We certainly need structures. What we do not need are structures of domination. No existing society, unless perhaps some hunter gatherer groups, is without such structures. Gandhi insisted that gaining independence was only the beginning of political freedom in India and was quite clear that true democracy is a goal which will always elude us but towards which we always have to strive.

Eusebius of Caesarea sang the praises of his hero Constantine, comparing him to Solomon. An apt comparison we might say, if we read the whole story, and if we see what Solomon's policies led to. If we let the story of Jesus of Nazareth act as our hermeneutical key, can we read the need for domination out of it? Christ 'did not regard equality with God as something to be hung on to, but emptied himself, taking the form of a slave' (Phil. 2.6). Those who want to defend it (which includes the senior managers of all Corporations) have to resort to what Niebuhr called 'Christian realism', which means only taking the gospel seriously so far. Ironically, Niebuhr's non-Christian contemporary, Gandhi, took it far more seriously, and with far greater effect.

Men are better equipped to dominate than women, some races than other races.

Let us begin with the second part of this proposition. Has not the South African struggle made clear once for all that as far as Scripture is concerned there can be no ground for fantasies of superior races? But what about patriarchy? Is not Scripture irredeemably patriarchal, as Mary Daly and Daphne Hampson argue? The proper reply to this is to point to the immense work of exegesis done by feminist Christian exegetes like Phyllis Trible, Elisabeth Schüssler Fiorenza, Elsa Tamez and many others which shows that service, and not domination, is at the heart of the whole gospel ethic. 'You know that among the Gentiles whose whom they recognise as their rulers lord it over them, and their great ones are tyrants over them. But it is not so among you.' (Mk. 10. 42-3) All kyriarchy (rule by bosses) is undermined by these words.

Violence is redemptive

Walter Wink speaks of violence as the spirituality of our age. He has in mind the Lone Ranger scenario, in which order is restored only by a good person with a gun. In Matthew we read - or at least Tolstoy, Gandhi and Martin

Luther King read: 'Do not resist an evildoer. But if anyone strikes you on the right cheek, turn the other also' (Mt. 5.38). Of course, the very way in which the death of Christ has been understood in the West has been an endorsement of redemptive violence, which has represented a failure to read the cross by the sermon on the mount, and vice versa.

Ruling or managing is the most important social function

I refer to Mark 10.43, part of the Church's founding charter. We can also instance Nietzsche here. He clearly has in mind the dialectic of the opening chapter of 1 Corinthians. which in turn springs from Paul's understanding of the cross. Despite his polemics, which imply that Christianity has won the day, it seems to me that the scandal of the prioritisation of the weak remains truly subversive of every social order in fact known to us. It is deeply counter intuitive to believe that, for example, the power of the World Bank and the IMF and the multi-national corporations can be challenged by a network of base communities without funding, and without much acceptance from their institutions. But were Paul writing today, this is clearly what he would be affirming. Nietzsche is right that this takes us to the heart of the gospel challenge.

Money is the most important value; property is sacred

In the Gospel we read: 'You cannot serve God and Mammon' (Mt. 6.24). In Acts we read: 'Now the whole group of those who believed were of one heart and soul, and no one claimed private ownership of any possessions, but everything they owned was held in common' (Acts 4.32). Of course, it is true that in Scripture, and especially in the Wisdom tradition, wealth is presented as a blessing and servants appear as part of that wealth. But these pictures have to be put in the context of the story of Naboth's vineyard, in which the land of Israel, which stands for the whole earth, is allocated to every family: every person under their vine and fig tree. Wealth in terms of money is never a value; fullness of life is a value. Money, the New Testament writers realised, threatens that fullness of life in radical ways (James 5.1-6).

Institutions are more important than people.

In the world in which Jesus lived, the Sabbath was probably the most important institution. It is indeed part of divine revelation, and something we should treasure, especially in relation to Sunday trading. But Jesus is quite c)ear: 'The sabbath is made for humankind; not humankind for the sabbath' (Mk. 2.27).

3. The Luzano Report

Self-interest is what motivates people.

I refer to the words about service in the Church's founding charter. We can of course reply that Jesus was a deluded fanatic who failed to understand what makes human beings tick. Or we can say that these words only apply to the converted, and not to the great mass of human beings who are 'inclined by nature to hate both God and their neighbour' in the amiable terms of the Heidelberg Catechism. I reply that Jesus' appeal to his disciples, based as it is on the Hebrew scriptures, presupposes the possibility of hearing and understanding.

The gospel of self-interest is diametrically opposed to the gospel of grace. It was a special coup of Satan that, when this gospel was re-discovered in the sixteenth century, it was almost at once privatised and individualised, linked exclusively to *my* salvation. But of course, as Jesus' parables make clear, grace is fundamentally about economics. If everything that we have and are is free and for nothing, if everything is the Lord's, then nothing is ours to hoard or corner, to amass capital with, to use to exclude or build hierarchies with. The reality of grace, as this appears in our Scriptures, is therefore profoundly subeversive of capital.

The free market is an instantiation of divine providence.

Strange as it may seem, there really are Christians who believe this bizarre doctrine (and not just pagans like Hayck). I counter by replying that the materials for a doctrine of providence in Scripture are all concerned with human flourishing, and especially the flourishing of the poor but, as Susan George has demonstrated time and again, the 'invisible hand' is not and cannot be. Market mechanisms systematically transfer wealth from the poor to the rich.

Social inequality is essential to human flourishing.

It is the opinion of the philosopher and ethicist Alisdair Macintyre that belief in equality is Christianity's major contribution to the world. Whether we look at the parable of the sheep and the goats or at the doctrine of the incarnation, we are reminded that all are sisters and brothers of the Human One ('Son of Man'). Although Christians through the ages have blithely connived in inequality, they can actually find no warrant for it from their Scriptures,

49

something which Levellers, Diggers and others had an inconvenient habit of reminding the 'great ones' of

Religions must stick to their proper concern and not interfere in politics.

This old chestnut appears time and again from politicians who are being challenged by the Church. I refer them to the Hebrew prophets. In the whole literature of the world's religions there are none which demand justice, mercy and truth in the way which these do, and none which so champion the poor and castigate the rich for injustice. In the Christian tradition we tend to take them for granted, but they are really a phenomenon. Where did they come from, these texts? How is it that they speak to us across the centuries with such power? Of course, they represent a reflection on the covenant traditions of Israel, particularly on what must be the case if God makes Godself known as the one who frees slaves. But the force with which they articulate the demands of justice is entirely their own, and they have without doubt shaped a whole way of thinking. We only have to look at the preaching of Ambrose and Chrysostum, and, and then the way in which their appeal to the prophetic texts is taken up by the medieval protest movements, and then by Levellers and Diggers, until it passes into the secular blood stream in the late eighteenth century, and from there enters the literature of the entire world. These are texts which are always, and will always be, deeply uncomfortable for the rich and powerful. The Sri Lankan theologian Aloysius Pieris, a Buddhist scholar, implacably opposed to any form of Christian triumphalism, nevertheless acknowledges that the unique thing about the Jewish and Christian scriptures is what he calls their emphasis on 'God's solidarity pact with the poor'[4] Managerial capitalism can only pretend it is consistent with Scripture by ignoring these texts.

The Bible, then, on my reading, is deeply subversive of the reigning axioms of the world in which we live. Having said this, there is the problem that we now live *in* a culture, in the West at least, where the Bible is not read. Undergraduates who come up to read Theology no longer know what is the Old Testament and what is the New. If you mention Moses and the prophets they will wonder if this is a new hip-hop group they have not yet heard of. Fifteen years ago the buzz word was 'intertextuality'. The Bible influences us, we sought to persuade ourselves, by shaping our culture. We 'indwell' the text. We can make sense of Ignatius Loyola or John Bunyan 'indwelling the text', but even if, in our culture, there are a few individuals or groups who seek to do this, we cannot possibly speak of it shaping a culture, subversively or any other way. Moreover, despite the protest of James Smart, we still have 'the strange silence of the Bible in the Church'. Lectionary readings, heard only on Sundays, are often presented in bite-size portions, out of context. In the Anglican Church, at least, many clergy leave out the Old Testament reading because they do not see its relevance; most 'preach' on the gospel. But what 'preaching' seems to mean is relating items of heart warming experience, the tenor of which is that it's nice to be nice. For those who try to read the Bible 'devotionally' (an idea which is surely opposed to every jot and tittle of Scripture) there are either guides whose purpose is to neuter the text, or, if we try to read without them, I expect that the experience of many is that of my eighty five year old mother. She frequently says to me: 'I read a bit every day. But I don't know *what* it's about!' She dutifully ploughs through Leviticus and Numbers, but the only harvest she reaps is puzzlement.

For the Bible to be subversive, then, the Church has to rediscover it. Rediscovering Scripture has always led to reformation and to challenges to the powers of the age. That is the task which awaits us.

---

[1] F. Nietzsche, The Anti-Christ. Harmondsworth: Penguin, 1968, p. 168

[2] W. Wink, Engaging the Powers. Minneapolis: Fortress, 1984, p.95/6

[3] S. George, The Lugano Report. London: Pluto, 1999, pp.27,55,61,75

[4] A. Pieris, An Asian Theology of Liberation. Edinburgh: T&T Clark, 1988

Joe Aldred and Garnet Parris

THE BIBLE AND THE BLACK CHURCH

1. Black Ministries in Britain

In this article we sketch out a perspective on the way in which Black Christians engage with the Bible. Of course, Black Christians in Britain are not concentrated in one church, we are spread out across the length and breadth of British denominationalism. Inevitably, when we write about Black Christianity in Britain, generalisations are used to convey a sense of what is going on. In the case of Black Christians and the Bible we recognise that there is a diversity of doctrinal traditions represented in the Black Christian community, but we perceive that there is also a 'Black love' of the Good Book that permeates denominational, traditional and cultural belongings. Such pervasive devotion is neither guarantee for consistency nor quality of interpretation of the Bible among Black Christians. This is so primarily because there is no ecclesiastical-doctrinal framework to which all Black Christians conform. What is presented here therefore, is reflective of the discourse among Black Pentecostalism in particular, less so of Black Christians in other traditions. We recognise that there is no 'one way' to interpret the Bible, rather that all Christian contexts, cultures and traditions, have a contribution to make to a holistic understanding of 'thus saith the Lord'. We start with a review of different hermeneutic methods before presenting some practical examples of resulting practice in the Black Church in Britain.

Black Christianity in Britain is characterised by a deep abiding love of the Bible as the unchallenged, authoritative Word of God to humanity. For example, when interviewed about their appreciation of the Bible some respondents said, "it is the breath I breathe"; another said, "I read it every day, it is my daily bread".[1] This unequivocal embrace which does not require formal biblical studies to affirm or authenticate it, has strengths and weaknesses, especially at a time when the Historical-Critical method is seen by many as scientific and a literalist/biblicist approach as pre-scientific. By and large Black-led churches have been characterised by a literalist approach, and yet this is not by any means exclusive to them. To the extent that this labelling is appropriate, the adoption of this tendency towards literalism can in part be attributed to Black Christians' and the Black-led churches' history of socio-economic disadvantage,[2] where those who occupy the pulpit have had little formal academic education which might have disposed them to a broader interpretative base. However times are 'a-changing' as more and more younger men and women with access to higher education occupy pulpits. However, because many British Black-led churches have links to headquarters with a fundamentalist or literalist approach to biblical interpretation, this approach may continue to enjoy prime status for some time. Neither is this simply a case of following orders, nor an excuse for a non-critical or pre-critical approach to the Bible, but it should be a matter of public record that Black-led churches have tended to provide their own internal schooling in matters of polity and doctrine. It has been easier to teach what was the denominational line rather than invite conflict.

However, Biblical usage among Black Christians and Churches is diverse. Three tendencies can be identified within the Black Church tradition: "Biblical literalism; eisegesis (the process of leading or reading into the text our own ideas):and the Black homily that conscientiously proceeds from exegesis to serious hermeneutical exposition".[3] The first two tendencies depend on proof-texting whereas the other is dependent on a critical posture that engages with the text in order to understand the issues it addressed then and to refocus on the issues to be addressed now. Within these the reality of the literal style and its respectability should not be consigned to the dustbin of history, because, for example, Black preaching is very much literal and action orientated and demands a literal response of faith and ethical living. It is understood in the kerygmatic preaching of Peter in Acts 2:37- 38, when Peter's audience, deeply troubled by the words they have heard asks, "What shall we do, brothers?" (GNB). Peter's response is in keeping with the Black preacher's understanding of the Word of God - 'Each one of you must turn away from your sins and be baptized in the name of Jesus Christ'.

This should be contrasted to the reality of those who had the knowledge, the tools, the education, but were found wanting in many respects when they closed their hearts and their churches to Black brothers and sisters during the mid-20th Century in Britain. The experience of many of the generation of the 1950s who first came to the UK is that biblical hermeneutics may have been technically 'correct' and diverse in terms of the approaches to the text, but it did not change lives in a godly manner. Many of the indigenous White preachers that they heard did not preach a word that was action oriented. Lives were not changed. And it was difficult to come to terms with a form of engaging the biblical text which seemed to be coldly intellectual, without warmth and lacking literal implications. Among Black Christians, there is still a sense of wonder, of confidence in believing that God has said it and it will come to pass. In attributing events, big and small, to the care and concern of God, the Black Christian acknowledges a God who is with us in all of life's triumphs and difficulties.

2. Sensus Plenior and Allegorisation

Even literal understandings can relate to some forms of interpreting the text which express concepts known as 'sensus plenior, spiritualizing, dehistoricizing and allegorizing'. The *sensus plenior* often indicates that a writer may be quite unaware of a deeper meaning found in their own writing, as seen in the statement, 'Out of Egypt I called my son' (Hos. 11:1); which although referring to the people of Israel, is seen by Matthew as having a fuller meaning that applies to the childhood of Jesus (Matt. 2:15). When it is suggested that the OT prophecies concerning the restoration of Israel should be understood in a spiritual sense, referring to the church, this is *spiritualizing*. We are involved in *dehistoricizing* when we view the story of Jonah as a parable intended to teach a lesson. And in the miracle at Cana, (John 2:1-11), the changing of water into wine, can be as symbolical of the need for those who are weak like water to be changed and become steadfast like wine – which is *allegorizing*. In some ways we may feel that allegorizing has a lot in common with *sensus plenior*. All of these approaches listed share one fundamental feature: they recognise that at certain points in the biblical text there appears to be 'something more' than is immediately apparent. This has to be understood within the wider context of the ability of the Spirit to teach all truth (John 16:13).

The charge that the Black Church uses the Bible in a way that is unusual when we allegorize, is interesting if we consider this sermon by John Chrysostom on the Gospel of John. In dealing with the wedding at Cana, he comments:
> At that time, therefore, Jesus made wine from water, and both
> then and now He does not cease changing wills that are weak
> and inconstant. Accordingly, let us bring to the Lord those
> who are thus disposed, so as to cause their will to change and
> become like wine, so that it no longer is inconstant, but
> steadfast, and they become a cause of rejoicing both for
> themselves and for others.[4]

Theodoret, the historical commentator, says about Isaac's reference to the dew from heaven and the fatness of the earth (Gen. 27:39):

> These things according to the obvious superficial sense of the letter denote grace from above and abundance of blessings from the earth; but according to the higher interpretation they depict the divinity of the Lord Christ by means of the expression dew; and by the fatness of the earth, his humanity received from us.[5]

Alongside an abiding concern for historical exegesis is a tension in which the allegorical interpretation remains as a constant thread in the understanding of the Bible. This tension can be demonstrated in the work of Rupert of Deutz,[6] for whom the letter gives instruction in holiness, but the mystical sense is a demonstration or prophecy of something far higher. Everywhere in Rupert's exegesis we can feel his consciousness of this lively tension between the literal and the spiritual senses, as he looks for the 'incorporeal and invisible' to come, which is foreshadowed by the 'corporeal and visible' deeds done in the past. The literal sense is a veil over the beauties which Grace reveals, and which a person must search for in the mirror of their sense-impressions.[7]

Although we would like to believe that these tensions were worked out in the Reformation with its strong emphasis on the literal sense of Scripture, we should remember that there were, for example, very conflicting views about the Lord's supper among the Reformers. There is still a debate that is raging about the way that Scripture should be understood, in that the question is asked as to whether we should be bound by the historical intent of the biblical author. Ricoeur places an emphasis on what he calls the 'reservoir of meaning' attached to all literary texts. The question 'What did the author mean?' is now regarded as still valid but largely uninteresting. The literary text, we understand, lives on after its author is dead, and so the ideas that later readers associate with the text can and must be viewed as part of its meaning. Although this point of view is a matter of considerable debate, broad segments of modern scholarship regard it as plausible and even respectable. However, what is to be noted here is that biblical scholarship,

> After triumphantly demonstrating that grammatico-historical exegesis is all that really matters, is being pressed on various sides to acknowledge that maybe there is something 'behind' or 'around' the text (at any rate, distinct from the original author's intent) that should be regarded as part of its meaning.[8]

We note that it was this aspect that was earlier thought to be totally unacceptable in the allegorical method, and for which today's Black Church is sometimes criticised. The allegorical method was not a quirk among early Christians nor need it be viewed as a pre-critical method among Black Christians. It should be viewed as one of the foundation stones in a large theological and intellectual edifice. We would argue that allegorical interpretations are very difficult to avoid for a believer who wishes to apply the truth of Scripture to his or her life. Such a concern is evident in the writings of Philo, who argued that there was no real point in reading about Abraham's journeys unless they refer to spiritual journeys in which we too participate.[9] Additionally, allegorizing is difficult to resist because the believer, quite naturally, expects the Word of God to say and do more than is immediately apparent. Clearly, it is not simply the literary power of allegory that appeals to a Christian congregation. Rather, a commitment to the divine inspiration of Scripture raises certain expectations in people's minds as to what they are likely to find in it.

Gerloff[10] suggests that the Black Church uses the Bible differently from the analytical approach of European Biblical theology, as it is a source for vision and inspiration, and a store-house for human conduct, attitudes and procedures. In fact we would suggest that attempts to say Black Christians part company in their use of the Bible with European Biblical theology brings a false dichotomy, as a history of the hermeneutical debate reveals that the Black church contributes to the reservoir of meaning within the Scriptures. There is a need for greater understanding of scientific methods as of other methods like literalist/biblicist, and the desire to allegorise and spiritualise is still paramount in a people who value the wisdom of learning verses of Scripture, so that the words of Scripture can be applied personally in times of need. The dangers that are inherent in a literalist/biblicist interpretative mould cannot be minimised. For we can sacrifice both the modern and the ancient contexts in which these sayings need to be understood in search of a spiritual or allegorical principle. In addition, as we seek spiritual principles, we can collude with aggressors and exploiters of the weak, thus, we can insist on a turning of the cheek when we are struck but seem to forget that the aggressor sometimes claims Christian principles in suuport of their actions. In a literalist/biblicist interpretative mould, we can sacrifice both the modern and the ancient contexts in which these sayings need to be understood in search of a spiritual or allegorical principle. In our need to seek spiritual principles we can collude with aggressors and exploiters of the weak, we can insist on a turning of the cheek when we are struck but seem to forget that the aggressor sometimes claims Christian principles too for their action. Yet, we can be honest about the way we can be encouraged by God's words, we can be humbled by its appropriateness for our situation and accept our shortcomings about making it applicable for a modern context.

In their strivings for biblical applicability, Black Christians need to be challenged by modern voices such as Beckford et al, that seek to point us to the debates about sexuality, politics, or social and racial justice. We need the rigours of background reading to understand the challenges that are contained in the first sermon of Jesus at the start of his public ministry in Luke 4:16-20. To understand that this message should be seen against the reality of Jubilee means that we are dealing with more than just spiritual realities. The challenge is to hear the word of God speak in the context of a world that is full of contradictions and complexities and which therefore requires a multifaceted hermeneutical approach to applying the truths of Scripture in it. It is this applicability to which we now turn.

3. Bible-Based Practice in Black Churches

Here we will share some practical examples of how Scripture is used to influence some specific practices, as a pointer to its use in general in Black-led churches in Britain. One example of the significance of the Bible and its hegemony in Black-led churches in Britain can be seen in the case of the Church of God of Prophecy,[11] whose position *viz a viz* the Bible is that it is the foundation upon which the organisation is built. To this end, everyone who is considered for membership has to accept the authoritative place of the Bible by affirming the following statement:

> Will you sincerely promise in the presence of God and these witnesses that you will accept this Bible as the Word of God, believe and practice its teachings rightly divided - the New Testament as your rule of faith and practice, government and discipline, and walk in the light to the best of your knowledge and ability? The answer is 'I will'.[12]

In this way, the Bible is located as the very pillar of the Church and of the individual. Another major influential factor behind the interpretation and application of Scripture is the near compulsive use of the King James Version as 'the' Bible. As one person was heard to say, 'if it was good enough for the Apostle Paul, it is good enough for me'. Pentecostals generally and the Black-led churches in Britain in particular, really do see the King James as the authentic version of the Bible. This embrace of seventeenth century language has contributed to some interesting hermeneutics, as in a literalist/biblicist mode, exegesis/homily vie with eisegesis resulting in 'sensus plenior', 'spiritualising', and allegorising of texts; all of which contribute to a way of using the Bible in Black-led churches and among Black Christians affected by these communities of faith. One of the more intriguing practices is that of 'tarrying'. This has two meanings in the traditional[13] Black-led church

57

experience: tarrying for the baptism of the Holy Spirit, and tarrying for one another at the communion table. The practice has its genesis in the Caribbean where in the early morning, tarrying services attracted seekers after the blessing of baptism. Bleary-eyed, people met as early as five a.m. to 'tarry' for the baptism of the Holy Spirit. These services can go on for many hours and are not confined to early mornings. It can be tarrying night services or all day fasting and tarrying services. Tarrying, however, does not simply mean waiting, it is primarily about praying long and hard whilst songs are sung, music is played and emotions run high until the climactic glossolalia bursts forth from the tarrying individual.

The exercise is based on Luke 24.49 "And, behold, I send the promise of my Father upon you: but tarry ye in the city of Jerusalem, until ye be endued with power from on high" (see also Acts 1.4). The disciples' instruction to wait in Jerusalem for empowerment for their mission of world evangelisation is understood quite literally and transcendently by the Black Pentecostal tradition as admonition to wait in similar fashion in every generation. In some Black-led church circles, tarrying for the Holy Spirit has lost intensity, and its passing or diminishing is greatly mourned by the elders. However, it can be argued that the idea of tarrying for the Holy Spirit is in some regards a disabling act. It suggests that the Holy Spirit has yet to come, rather than building on the experience of the earlier disciples. Also, it suggests that the reality of the Spirit in the life of the believer is subject to the human experience of glossolalia.

The second act of tarrying takes some fathoming for the uninitiated. In the heyday of the traditional Black Church, and still sometimes today, people gathered for the Lord's Supper (Communion) with communicants dressed in White. There was a table draped also in White; and after a sermon warning that those who dare to eat and drink of the Lord's table unworthily, eat and drink damnation to themselves, those who felt worthy to partake come forward and were seated. Behind them, a second line gathered, adopting a kneeling position. It was these who were tarrying. Unlike the tarrying for the baptism of Holy Spirit, these are merely awaiting their turn to partake of the Lord's Supper. The biblical justification for this is 1 Cor. 11.33 "Wherefore, my brethren, when ye come together to eat, tarry one for another". Here the use of the King James' language is significant since most other translation render the word 'wait'. This text is dehistoricised in a manner that calls out for the application of, say, the historical-critical method of hermeneutic. The concept of the Corinthian 'love feast' becoming the travesty of the rich providing and enjoying sumptuous portions of food to the point of over-eating and drunkenness, while the poor and the slaves were still making their way to the service, if indeed they got there at all, is quite lost in this practice of tarrying. The meaning of a text which speaks powerfully of the need to confront inequalities and wanton disregard of the less off by the rich is lost in this meek, if exhibitionist, interpretation. The kneeling that waits for its turn to partake of the Lord's Supper might be more liberating if its practitioners focussed on action to level up the social, political and economic, even spiritual, differentials between fellow partakers. It could be argued though, in the application of 'sensus plenior', that the symbolism of waiting on one's knees acts as a reminder to wait on, or be patient towards one another in the hustle-bustle of daily life.

4. Personal Practice and Biblical Rules

Until quite recently, and still in many Black Church settings, the way Christians, particularly women, dressed has been a deeply divisive issue. The key scriptural drivers are 1 Tim. 2:9 where the Greek *kosmeo* means to put in order, or decorate; and 1 Peter 3:3 where the Greek *kosmos* means orderly arrangement, or decoration. In these texts to 'adorn' conveys positive, not negative, overtones. However, in both cases it is the negative that gets the emphasis in the Black-led churches, so that the second section of 1 Tim. 2:9 is emphasised:"not with braided hair, or gold, or pearls, or costly array". The women are instead instructed to "adorn themselves in modest apparel, with shamefacedness and sobriety (and) with good works" (1 Tim. 2:9a & 11). This emphasis has led to great stress upon the way women in the church dress, with 'high enough neckline, low enough hemline' being the stated, or unstated, standard. The traditional position adopted by these churches is summed up well by Mathew Henry when he says, "Women who profess the Christian religion should be modest, sober, silent, and submissive".[14] This would undoubtedly be hotly challenged by many women. Very recently in a local church the wearing of a sleeveless dress to church by a sister was the subject of ministerial discussion. Of course were we to go back a little earlier, 'backless' shoes for women and shorts or short trousers for men were out too! It is difficult to find any redeeming feature in these prohibitions. They pander to exhibitionism in the attempt to demonstrate holiness of life, and at another level they oppress the expressiveness of women to enhance and exhibit their external beauty. While gaudiness and extremism in adornment is to be modified, it is surely wrong to assume that beautifying the outer means that one is not also beautifying the inner, or that not beautifying the outer means that you are beautiful inside. Holistically, both inner and outer adornment are necessary for the individual, with the need to achieve balance and moderation left to the individual living with the constraints, restraints, and cultural expectations of their religious community. The eisegesis involved in exclusionary teachings about adornment might benefit from exegesis on moderation which would have far-reaching consequences well beyond clothing and jewellery!

Probably the most severe interpretation in terms of what is worn is reserved for jewellery. Based largely upon 1 Peter 3:3 women have been forbidden to straighten their hair or wear any form of jewellery, including in the case of at least one denomination, a wedding ring.[15] This is based upon the text which says, "Whose adorning let it not be that outward adorning of plating the hair, and of wearing of gold, or of putting on of apparel" (1 Peter 3:3). These must be sacrificed and in their place comes a meek and quiet spirit (1 Peter 3:4). The woman's beauty must be an inner attribute, not one that is achieved by outward adorning. Grudem makes the salient point that the Greek text does not include an adjective that modifies clothing. The conclusion therefore is that if one uses the text to prohibit women from braiding their hair or wearing gold jewellery, by the same reasoning one would have to prohibit the 'putting on of apparel'.[16]

Sometimes these applications of biblical texts have devastating consequences. For example, the requirement for women to remove their wedding rings to become members of a church has broken up marriages and opened some wives to abuse from their husbands, family members and, tellingly, when they have gone into hospitals to have children. Many have testified to being disrespected by some hospital staff who assumed them to be unmarried mothers. It would of course not be right to discriminate against unmarried mothers, but the treatment is made worse when the woman is married. Some believed they were suffering for the Gospel, others put their ring on during their hospital stay, unable to allow their hand to surface whilst members and especially the minister visit.

There is now a tension between many women and some men and their churches that have come to disregard these prohibitions, but this disregard is not tolerated in all churches. Where jewellery wearing is permitted or tolerated in the traditional Black-led churches, some among those who lived through the days of prohibition feel let-down, cheated and hurt at having suffered to abide by their church's teachings only now to find the teachings no longer upheld. There is a break with these traditions by the new Black-led churches springing up around England which adopt a more liberal interpretative posture towards adornment, for example. It remains to be proven whether this development leads to a departure from the literalist/biblical approach.

5. Alcohol and Bishops

Another example of the way in which Black-led churches interpret Scripture is their attitude towards alcoholic beverages. The near universal line is 'total abstinence from all liquor and strong drinks'. This means that all beverages with any amount of alcohol are forbidden. Biblical justification is found in texts such as Prov. 20:1 "Wine is a mocker, strong drink is raging, and whosoever is deceived thereby is not wise". Prov. 23:29-30 "Who hath woe? Who hath sorrow? Who hath contentions? Who hath babbling? Who hath wounds without cause? Who hath redness of eyes? They that tarry long at the wine; they that go to seek mixed wine." Add to these stark warnings Paul's admonitions not to keep company with drunkards (1 Cor. 5:11), his assertion that drunkards will not inherit the kingdom of God (1 Cor 6.10 & Gal 5.21); and a very strong case can be made for total abstinence from such a potentially dangerous substance. Contemporary uses of alcohol that lead to violence, rowdiness, abuse, road accidents, et al, may also support the Black-led churches' literalist stance.

However, literalism is not a euphemism for inadequate observation and analysis. It is clear that what these texts condemn is drunkenness, less so all indulgence, the fear of which might legitimise 'total abstinence'. It has been argued that total abstinence is a failsafe mechanism for ensuring against drunkenness. The practice of some Black Christians demonstrate that they are unconvinced about the teaching. Some consumption of 'alcohol' is evident in for example the practice of putting wine in cakes and cooking. There is evidence that at many weddings nowadays, alcoholic drinks are also provided and consumed, plus the occasional popping of champagne corks at celebratory events such as anniversaries or birthdays. A member of a Black-led church admitted that he rarely goes to bed without consuming a can of beer, in spite of what his church teaches. It can be regarded as rather strange that Spirit-filled Christians, for whom temperance (Gal. 5:23) is a much-vaunted fruit, need to resort to total abstinence in order to avoid drunkenness.

Recently, a Bishop in an effort to drive home the priority of total abstinence said, 'if you drink two glasses of 5% that makes 10%'. Whenever mention is made of texts that appear to support consumption of anything alcoholic, the hermeneutic of ridicule is deployed. So, pointers to Jesus' miracle of turning water into wine at the wedding feast at Cana (John 2:1-11) and Paul's admonition to "drink no longer water, but use a little wine for thy stomach's sake and thine often infirmities" (1 Tim. 5:23), are met with, 'do you really believe that Jesus would have made alcoholic wine for people to get drunk on?' We have already alluded to one possible allegorical interpretation. And of course, the notion of using wine for medicinal purposes is ruled out completely, in the face of many from the Caribbean being convinced that a little White rum works wonders in ridding oneself of a cold. One of the challenges faced by our Black students at the Centre for Black and White Christian Partnership who come from Pentecostal backgrounds, is whether to partake of communion in churches which use alcoholic wine for communion on our monthly visits. Black-led churches would benefit from a biblical hermeneutic that supports moderation, even while it continually warns of the dangers of over-consumption that can lead to drunkenness and its dire consequences. Again though, it can be argued that these churches' unyielding literalist line, though now being challenged, has shielded many from the destructive consequences of strong drink. Whether the end justifies the means in hermeneutical terms is debatable.

1 Tim. 3:2 says, "A bishop then must be blameless, the husband of one wife, vigilant, sober, of good behaviour, given to hospitality, apt to teach". Within some denominations this has been interpreted as requiring a bishop to be both male and married, and this must be his only marriage unless he was widowed. In line with Black-led churches' interpretation, Adam Clarke says, "He should be a married man, but he should be no polygamists; and have only one wife, i.e.,one at a time. It does not mean that, if he has been married and his wife dies, he should never marry another".[17] There appears to be a fear of recognising the possibility of the polygamous lifestyle of the community to which this was written, lest it gives licence to those who might want to legitimise such arrangements in our day. More so, it would accept that polygamy has been part of the Christian experience. A reasonable reading of this text however seems to suggest that what was being stated here was a stance against polygamy for those who would aspire to the high office of bishop, rather than insisting upon a precedent that one had to be married.

In recent times in Britain, there has been some breaking down of the male only rule for those who would be bishop. In one Oneness Pentecostal denomination, there is a female bishop, and a female Archbishop in an African Initiated Church in London. The effects of a strict interpretation of "must be male and married" results in exclusion for some whose calling makes them suitable for oversight work but who are neither male nor married, or if married have been married before. This does not apply in some churches that do not permit second marriages for any other reason other than the death of a spouse. This has led also to circumstances where less suitable people in terms of their gifting and calling assume posts which would be better suited for others who are disqualified on the above technicalities. This interpretation calls into question also some received understandings. For example, Jesus is recognised as Head, the Bishop in Chief of the Church, and "Shepherd and Bishop of your souls" (1 Peter 2:25), yet he never married. Paul, the person credited with many of the writings used to arrive at these understandings, was an overseer and apostle, yet arguably was not married. Could Paul have invented a policy which disqualified himself even whilst he held the position?

6. Empowering Texts

If some literal biblical interpretations oppress and exclude people, some positively empower them. The statement, "But ye shall receive power, after that the Holy Spirit is come upon you" (Acts 1:8a), acts as a catalyst for Black Pentecostals in a way that exceeds the notion of being witnesses, i.e., preachers of the Gospel. Individuals, who had been timid and withdrawn, inside and outside church, lay claim to supernatural power after experiencing glossolalia. With the Holy Spirit on the inside, they are not afraid of anybody or anything on the outside. Black Christians often cast themselves in the mould of the early disciples such as Peter and John who were deemed "unlearned and ignorant" (Acts 4:13), yet able to accomplish supernatural feats that baffled the 'wise'. In a recent sermon, the preacher emphasised the meaning of the word 'power' as it is used in Acts 1:8. He highlighted its Greek derivative *dunamis* which means miraculous power, strength, violence and might, as the term from which the English 'dynamite' is derived. It is precisely this kind of explosive power that Black Pentecostals believe they receive when the Holy Spirit comes upon them.

However, this ideology is not without its downside also. We have already alluded to the practice of tarrying for the baptism of the Holy Spirit. In traditional Pentecostal churches, one of the consequences of not receiving the baptism with the evidence of glossolalia is that people are viewed as not having this dynamic power. The churches largely ignore the Pauline rhetorical question, "do all speak with tongues?" (1 Cor. 12:30), in favour of the Lukan account that "they were all filled with the Holy Spirit, and began to speak with other tongues" (Acts 2.4). Among other things, the 'not filled' ones may be viewed as unsuited for spiritual office. This has tended to create a first and second class pecking order in Black-led Pentecostal churches. It appears inconceivable that some Christians can have access to a power source that others have not. A hermeneutic that affirms this may be helpful.

Another liberating understanding derived from a literalist interpretation concerns the catholicity of the Christian Church, in which all Christians *are* one: not going to be, but are. It is Galatians 3:28 that forms the scriptural basis of this understanding. The restoration of fallen humanity in

Jesus Christ is interpreted by Black Christians to mean that whatever they may or may not posses in material terms, however much 'the world' may consider them inferior, they consider themselves at one, equal with, all other Christians. In sermons, testimonies and songs, this community affirms that whether they have thick or thin lips, kinky or straight hair, brown or blue eyes, whether they are tall or short, female or male, Black or White, Asian, African, Caribbean or European - all are one in Christ. Whilst this is empowering enough, we think there are some possible downsides too. Given the context in which some Black people have imbibed notions of being inferior to Whites, and where some Whites have equally imbibed notions of being superior, it is possible that what is going on is that Blacks believing Whites to be superior may be glorying in becoming equal to their superiors through the Church. Also, we detect some signs of negative Black appropriation of oneness when some, particularly educated and professional, Blacks leave the Black-led churches to join White-led ones, on the basis that as we are all one it does not matter where they worship. Of course what may be happening is that they are aligning themselves with White ways of being church and distancing themselves from the ecclesiology of the largely oral tradition of the Black-led churches. Clearly it is insufficient to embrace a simplistic understanding of oneness. A complex ideology requiring a complex hermeneutic to apply it.

The final example we give here the belief that Jesus is head of the Church. This has led, in some Black-led churches, to the reply, 'my church's headquarters are in heaven', when asked where their headquarters are. Using the allegory of the marriage institution, where the man is said to be the head of the marriage household, Eph. 5:23 posits Christ as head of the church (Eph. 5:23). Being answerable to the invisible Christ has led to some indisciplined proliferation among Black-led churches, as well as some healthy disregard for traditional institutions which would want to restrict the manoeuverability of churches that operate independently of them. In Britain since the 1950s, for example, Black church leaders have felt completely at ease setting up churches without reference to the existing 'mainstream' ones. Their understanding has been that they are working under the direct authority of Christ, head of the catholic church. They recognise no other authority or lord but The Lord and have determined that relationships are possible only on the basis of mutual respect as sister churches, not on the basis of a mainstream which views the minority as a bastardised version of the real thing.

In summary, Black-led churches, indeed Black Christians everywhere, see the Bible as God's Word to them and to the world. As we have been demonstrating, the hermeneutics of these churches are not always liberating.

Quite apart from the limited ground that we have covered in this essay, women may argue that they in particular have been the butt of improper use of Scripture. In a recent anthology by Black British Christian women, several depict the church in general and the Black-led churches in particular as oppressive places, where Scripture is interpreted in manifold ways that discriminate against women.[18] On the whole, however, the Bible remains a liberating tool within the Black-led churches and will continue to be so, as that community broadens its interpretative methodologies, without lessening the primacy of the position of the Bible in their midst.

---

[1] JD Aldred, A Black Majority Church's Future. unpublished thesis, University of Sheffield, 1994.

[2] C. Hope Felder, Troubling Biblical Waters. Maryknoll, NY: Orbis, 1989 p.79.

[3] Ibid. p. 88.

[4] Moises Silva, Has the Church Misread the Bible? Vol 1, p.53.

[5] Ibid. p. 54.

[6] Rupert of Deutz, c.1075 – 1129: Medieval theologian and exegete.

[7] Moises Silva, Has the Church Misread the Bible? Vol, p. 55.

[8] Moises Silva, Has the Church Misread the Bible? Vol 1, p. 57.

[9] Samuel Sandmel, Philo of Alexandria, ANRW 2.25. 2. pp. 227-71 Moises Silva, Has the Church Misread the Bible? Vol 1, p. 63.

[10] RIH Gerloff, A Plea for British Black Theologies. Frankfurt am Main: Peter Lang, 1992, p.13.

[11] It is worth remembering that the Church of God of Prophecy like some other Black-led churches in Britain, borrows its basic doctrinal position from White-led American Pentecostal-Holiness traditions.

[12] 90th General Assembly Minutes and Policy Manual. Church of God of Prophecy, Cleveland, Tennessee, USA, 1998, p. 242.

[13] By traditional is meant those Black-led churches that were planted in Britain since the 1950s by people from the Caribbean and Africa. These have different emphases and practice from newer churches which in many cases have emerged in response to the desire to throw off some old practices.

[14] Matthew Henry, The Bethany Parallel Commentary on the New Testament. Minneapolis:Bethany House Publishers, 1983. p.1232

[15] After much protestation, and eventual near rebellion, the Church reluctantly permitted the wearing of wedding rings since 1989.

[16] Wayne Grudem, Tyndale New Testament Commentaries. Leicester:Inter-Varsity Press, 1988, p. 140

[17] Adam Clarke, The Bethany Parallel Commentary. Minnesota: Bethany House Publishers, 1983, p. 1233.

[18] See Joe Aldred, Ed., Sisters with Power. London:Continuum, 2000.

Ian K. Duffield

FROM BIBLE TO MINISTRY PROJECTS

1. A UTU Process

From 1983 to 1988, the Urban Theology Unit was the UK base for the Doctor of Ministry Programme of New York Theological Seminary. From 1991 to the present UTU has run its own Master/Doctor of Ministry programme validated by the University if Sheffield. Dr John Vincent was Director of both NYTS and Sheffield MMin/DMin programmes until 1997, with myself as Associate, and I have been responsible for the programme since 1997. Out of this, 34 theses were completed for the NYTS DMin. To May 2001, we have had 31 Sheffield MMin graduates, and so far one DMin.

This is the experience out of which I write about the Bible leading to ministry projects. The 66 completed theses constitute a significant witness to what follows, and illustrate the method in a wide variety of contexts and applications.

2. A Method

Serious engagement with the scriptures is integral to Christian ministry. In our postgraduate programmes which focus on ministry at the Urban Theology Unit, we have for many years explored a discernment process to assist candidates and congregations to correlate their particular situation with the Bible as a means to assisting and developing contemporary practice with a specific project in ministry.[1] What follows is based on course material developed by ourselves at UTU for use in the Master/ Doctor of Ministry programmes.

The first step in the process is the formation of a small group of people who work together, the "Site Team", in the DMin jargon. They begin by analyzing their current ministerial situation in all sorts of ways. This draws upon practical experience, statistical data, historical records, and observation. In particular, the group is asked to ascertain the key *joys* and *sorrows* of both their congregation and the community in which they are set--whether it be a small neighbourhood, a housing estate, market town, city centre, or region. From this "Situation Analysis" of their particular context, they are invited to engage in a mutual exploration of some biblical passages that appear to have some particular relevance or resonance to their faith community in its background setting. The search is for 'suggestive stories' and 'evocative parallels' which will in some measure correlate with their own experience and struggle, for an 'imaginative identification', as John Vincent[2] calls it, between ourselves, our contexts and our possible actions, and biblical ones.

In a specific, current context, the Bible as a whole is not helpful – only particular passages, people, or themes are. It is wrong to think that every biblical passage or verse is helpful in any particular situation as it is to think that no biblical text could be of any use. Discrimination and discernment are required. This can be the most difficult part off correlating the Bible with a ministerial context. What passages are *for us* in this context? Often this is not immediately obvious. Sometimes passages that might seem to correlate, because of similar language or traditional use, are not helpful. A superficial correspondence of terms needs to be replaced by what Clodovis Boff calls, a 'Correspondence of relationships'.[3]

There are various ways in which this search can be conducted. My colleague, Robin Pagan, has developed a brief guide to contextual bible study that provides an imaginative way into considering social, economic, and political aspects of passages in relation to identified concerns:

3. A Step-by-Step Guide

- Step 1.   Brain storm concerns arising from analysis of the situation and define specific themes. (Brainstorming encourages participants to contribute the first thing that comes to mind. It is important that even so-called 'silly' suggestions are not filtered out because they can provide the most fruitful point of departure. It is important to record all suggestions with the use of a flip chart or the like.) Prefer concrete to abstract definition, e.g. 'valley' rather than 'depression', 'door' rather than 'opportunity', 'bridge' rather than 'communication', etc.
- Step 2.   Choose the most significant definitions/themes, say two or three, and find biblical references using a concordance with a good range of references.

- Step 3.   Differentiate   between   helpful/appropriate   and unhelpful/inappropriate passages and choose one or two for further investigation.
- Step 4.   Leader researches into socio-economic, political context of the passages chosen in Step 3. Work out contending parties both explicit and implicit within the biblical text.
- Step 5.   Role play biblical situation chosen and researched. Divide into contending groups analyzed and hand out research material collected in Step 4 so that each group can play out their role with conviction. Encourage those with some biblical experience to use it within the requirements of the exercise.
- Step 6.   Make sure that the members of the group are brought out of role, so that their identification with their character is brought to an end. Then discuss insights gained: a)   into the biblical passage with particular reference to its socio-economic and political aspects in its original context. b)   into implications of passage for original concerns arising from your situation analysis.

Obviously, the discernment process is facilitated by a wide-ranging knowledge of the scriptures. However, even groups that are relatively new to faith can engage in such an exploration. The advice and assistance of others with experience in this way of working can be helpful in stimulating the process and in suggesting passages and ideas to explore on the basis of the analysis of the situation that has been worked at beforehand. In this kind of exploration, we have found that the use of experimental and participatory modes of bible study are particularly effective, such as role play (see above). Those who lead such groups need to familiarize themselves with such methods (such as those advocated by Walter Wink[4]), which are still relatively unknown. These methods assist those not familiar with the scriptures, and enables those who know their scriptures to engage with them in a new and stimulating way.   Such creative bible study assists in demarcating how relevant, or not, certain passages are to the particular situation within which the people have to live.

It is important to realize that such working with the Bible is not limited to specialists or those with degrees. Creative engagement with scripture in such groups can lead to authentic discoveries and practical action.   This is unlikely if approached in a narrowly academic manner or with a 'primary naiveté' that accepts everything in scripture at face value. As Robert McAfee Brown[5] says, those who have subjected the scripture to critical scrutiny need to approach biblical passages with a 'secondary naiveté' that returns to the text as it stands, and asks, 'What does this passage say to us?'   Furthermore, it is important, in the words of Jorge Pixley[6], to 'read the ideas of the Bible in terms of the historical struggles of flesh-and-blood people'. Because there is so much 'idealism' and 'lack of realism' in religious circles, these are very important matters in helping to get the most help from scripture in developing practice.

Discovering the Problem

On the basis of the original analysis of the situation, together with this biblical exploration, the group is then asked to identify the *key* issue or problem in their location that needs addressing. In some so-called 'comfortable' settings a precise problem proves difficult to articulate. In some so-called 'needy' areas there are too many problems so that it becomes hard to focus on one. This can be a difficult step in this method. Even if a problem appears to be obvious, its articulation in a clear and precise manner often proves elusive. We are so used to speaking in a general and imprecise way. But essential to a practical project in ministry is the clear delineation of a problem in a specific way: names have to be named, realities have to be described in an accurate way. Often there is a deeper problem beneath the presenting one. Sometimes, people know the problem but only in a vague way. The problem needs definition, and sometimes the biblical experience can help to articulate it.

Furthermore, it is often from a biblical perspective that we can see that one problem rather than another needs addressing. In other words, the scriptures can provide us with a sense of urgency with regard to particular kinds of problems. For example, there are certain kinds of problem within the household of faith that need attention, and may have to be dealt with before focusing on more external matters. In terms of a practical project in ministry, it is important for the problem that is addressed to be one that merits significant attention from some biblical perspective. That are many problems that may be addressed, but why this one? Relating study of the Bible to our particular situation can help us distinguish greater from lesser issues.

Clear definition of problem assists clear definition of task, that is action. Practice which seeks to take seriously the particularities of a particular location must articulate the reality clearly. Practice which seeks to be Christian needs to see that what it is tackling has some correspondence to what the People of God have tackled before, in whatever different circumstances and with different resources.

4. Biblical Paradigms and Antecedents

Of course, for Christians, their supreme resource is God, beyond that is the community of faith, made up of people, just like the People of God in its various manifestations throughout the biblical period. It is the Bible, supremely, which articulates for us who and how God is and, therefore, who and how God is now. It is also the Bible, preeminently, which articulates for us the nature and character of the People of God within a wide variety of setting and conditions from slavery to freedom. In our contemporary world-- where people often find themselves as minorities or experiencing oppression of some form, or the problems of leadership and office, or the difficulties of an ethnically diverse community--the Bible can be a resource for what it means to be the People of God in our differing contexts. Thus, we search for Paradigms or Antecedents in the biblical narratives, which appear to relate to our own contemporary realities.

Certain parts of the Bible seem to be more available as paradigms or antecedents to particular people at particular times. Liberation Theology has identified the Exodus as a fruitful paradigm for oppressed peoples in the Third World. This is less likely to be useful in other situations. From my experience of working with ministers, in the UK, in making connections between the Bible and the contemporary practice of ministry[1], I would identify the following trends:

- the Old Testament is more likely to be found useful than the New Testament
- narratives are preferred to theology
- the period of Exile and Restoration is often referred to
- parables are the most preferred passages from the New Testament
- Metaphors and concrete symbols, such as 'tent' and 'body', are more likely to be used than abstract notions.

The issues of establishing identity, formation of community, and dealing with boundaries are fairly common in ministers seeking to engage with contemporary realities of communal and church life. From this has come the above interest in the period of the Restoration after the Exile and the prophets associated with that period. Very different ministers in contrasting locations have found themselves dealing with this period of the Hebrew Scriptures. For example, Br Stephen Smyth seeking to support Roman Catholic Teachers under pressure in the East End of Glasgow and Stephen Owens, an Anglican Vicar in the West Midlands working to improve the relationship between the church, the local community, and the Showmen (who have their quarters adjacent to the church) and has turned to Third Isaiah (56-66) for illumination.[7]

The following section gives some recent ministry project examples of the different kinds of relationship between a variety of ministerial contexts, biblical passages and practice.

5. Five Examples[8]

Creating a Vision for Great Yarmouth[9]

Canon Michael Woods is the Team Rector in the Anglican Parish of Great Yarmouth. Since the late 1960s, he says, "a decline in the holiday industry, and the disappearance of the fishing industry, have combined to create a serious problem. A town which once saw itself clearly as a port and holiday resort has lost its sense of purpose."[10] This lack of vision, he determined with others, was dangerous for the future of the town.

Groups of people in the town were brought together to seek to express a vision. This was "tempered with biblical insights concerning what makes for a good community."[11] This 'Vision Document' was communicated to the decision-makers of the town and has resulted in a new self-image for Great Yarmouth. Among the biblical material that proved important were the biblical themes of vision and dream (pp.68ff). The Isaianic oracle requiring God's people to be inclusive (Isa 56:3-8) was found to be significant (pp.219f). Also certain parables were resources for their 'Vision Document' (pp.138ff): the parable of the talents (Mt 25:14-30); Lk 19:12-27), the two builders (Mt 7:24-27; Lk 6:47-49), and the sheep and the goats (Mt 25:31-46).

Developing a Multi-Racial Church in Suburban London[12]

All Saints', a south London parish, began to realise that as a "predominantly middle-class, comfortable, semi-eclectic, suburban parish church" it was not fully reflecting "the diverse and ever changing local community" in Upper Norwood, and needed help "to cope with the dynamics of change in the period of transition from a predominantly white congregation to a black and white congregation."[13]

The Vicar, Alan Middleton, with others, identified three biblical antecedents to their situation (pp.93ff & 187ff). They "discerned a parallel between the situation in Isaiah 11:1-3a with the shoot, the stump and the branch, and the situation that we felt that we were in at All Saints'. We could not help but feel that we were on the verge of something new."[14]   Another Isaiah text concerning the acceptance and welcoming of strangers, Isa 56:1-8 was considered to be pertinent (pp.96ff & 192ff), and identified as a reversal of Deut 23:3,6 (p.100).   The third antecedent was seen in Jer 30:12-17, which was a promise of restoration (pp.103ff & 197ff).   These words gave "great hope" because they emphasised that "newness comes only the presence of explicit grief."   They concluded: "Our own grief at the state of affairs needed to lead on to a renewal of our future."   This would include a warm welcome "to all members of the ethnic minority groups in our area."[15]

As a result of this project in ministry, ethnic minorities now play a fuller part in church life and All Saints' has been transformed into a multiracial congregation and has become more representative of the local community.

Clarifying the Role of Industrial Chaplain in Birmingham[16]

Trevor Lockwood is Industrial Chaplain with the NEC Group in Birmingham, which includes the famous National Exhibition Centre.   In his project he sought to deal with the tension between the pastoral and prophetic roles that were endemic to his position.   Obviously, from a biblical point of view, consideration was given to the role of a prophet and various categories were identified: founder/prophet (p.76), judge/prophet (p.77), priest/prophet (p.78). How the prophetic role was exercised was examined (pp.79ff) and those were identified "who exercised their ministry with the royal circle, the 'court' prophets, who were with the king and possessed a relationship with him which enabled them to act in a different way."[17]   Nathan was identified as a good example of a court prophet and this raised various issues of power (pp.81ff). This led to parallels being made with the relationship between the Chaplain to the NEC Group and the Company Chief Executive.   The pastoral role was also considered (pp.89ff) with reference to the biblical image of the shepherd in, for example, John 10:14-16 and Luke 15:4-7.   From the group who studied these passages emerged the notion of 'pastoring the organisation' (pp.101ff). It was concluded that although the two roles of pastor and prophet possess an inherent tension that cannot be avoided, they are not mutually exclusive but rather are to be understood as complementary (p.97).

Through the project the Chaplain "became increasingly recognised as an important part of the Company structure and culture."[18]   In biblical terms, the role of the Chaplain has been clarified: in terms of a prophetic role he is something of a court prophet; and in terms of a pastoral role he is developing the notion of 'pastoring the organisation', which has added a new dimension to the development of Industrial Mission at the beginning of a new century.

Struggling with Meaning in a Comfortable Derbyshire Village[19]

Methodists in the middle-class Derbyshire village of Duffield realised that they needed a new sense of purpose and direction. It was later discerned that there was a problem of privilege. Surprisingly, the Book of Job emerged as a text which resonated--not Job himself, but his so-called 'friends' (pp.26ff, cf. 220f): "We realised that affluent, comfortable, secure Duffield had something in common with Job's friends, who preached their traditional theology to Job when they did not really understand his suffering."[20] Like Job's friends, they were "comfortable and secure, distant from the struggles of the rest of the population"; they were "a village where 'well-to-do' people hid their suffering, either not liking to acknowledge it, or believing that they, the powerful, were able to deal with it by themselves."[21]

Alison Geary, the Methodist Minister, realized that this linkage with the Book of Job was, fundamentally, an intuition (p.227), but one she could not escape from. Her continuing sense of surprise, even shock, comes through when she writes: "The paradox of this affluent, comfortable, secure village in the white highlands of Derbyshire linking itself with the Book of Job is extraordinary."[22] But this biblical antecedent helped provide a profound way through the presenting problem: "Job found meaning and integrity when he moved beyond the friends' traditional theology, so listening to the 'Jobs' of today might help Duffield to find a new purpose and direction to solve the problem of meaninglessness. As the Job narrative makes clear, a meaningful and integrated theology is ultimately determined by the way questions of suffering are dealt with."[23]

Migrating the Church in Chapeltown, Sheffield[24]

Two Methodist Societies in Burncross and Chapeltown, in Sheffield, had to leave their old chapels to build a new common church at the centre of the community in Chapeltown. This physical migration which was already planned came to be understood in a new light. It was a profound shock to the Minister, Keith Lackenby, to find these congregations relating to a rather unfamiliar part of the Old Testament. They found themselves considering the two traditions of the Tabernacle in Exodus 25-40 (pp.74ff): "the elaborate Tabernacle of the 'P' Tradition and the more simple Tent of Meeting of the 'E' Tradition."[25]

This had a profound impact upon them and how they conducted their migration. "The portable and impermanent nature of the Tabernacle was to provide a catalyst in our theological thinking. Reflection on the important

73

things we wished to preserve and which we place in the 'Tent' at the final service in Burncross related tot he spiritual life of the church not its physical structure."[26] Worship material for final act of worship at Burncross utilized material from Exodus 25-30 & 35-40. After the reading of Exodus 26 members of the Girls Brigade and the Boys Brigade pitched a tent in the centre of the chapel. Then, symbolically, members wrote on a piece of paper what they wanted to take with them to the new church, e.g. 'prayer', 'friendship'. At the conclusion, the tent that contained what they wanted for their physical and spiritual pilgrimage was packed away to be taken to where the tent was to be pitched in Chapeltown, when all the pieces of paper where displayed on the walls of the new church (p.108). Theological insights inspired by the 'Tabernacle' engendered a new understanding of sacred space for them as Methodists.

In the transitional period from the old chapels to the new church it was the journey of the people of God in the wilderness years that provided an important perspective (p.94). In this migration they "faced the tension between the Temple which endures from generation to generation and the Tent of Meeting which is carried by the Pilgrim people of God to be pitched in the wilderness camp of human life."[27] Although there was this strong emphasis on Exodus, the significance of John 1:14 and Christ's 'tabernacling among us' brought a deeper awareness of the incarnation (pp.82f & 172f) and the 'tabernacling' of the Christian community in their new church in the community of Chapeltown.

6. The Relationship between Bible and Practice

The relationship between Bible and practice in these examples is very varied. The Bible, in each case, does not fulfill the same function. Often, people will look at numerous passages. Some will provide insight and challenge. Others will be looked at seriously and studied in depth only to be set aside as not useful at this particular juncture. Passages can come across very powerfully but not have that much impact on practice. Other times, a text may be regarded as relevant but not powerful and yet have a hidden influence of a profound kind on what happens.

Biblical passages, themes, or people that provided paradigms and antecedents for us emerge in differing ways. Sometimes it is the fruit of disciplined study, other times it is as the result of an intuition or an unplanned comment. Sometimes it emerges early on, other times in the midst of engagement or even afterwards. In other words, the Bible can have an impact at each of the three moments of practice: (a) in the consideration of what should be done and how it should be done; (b) during engagement with action; (c) as a matter of reflection after practice.

Although, in this article, I have stressed the first moment, the other two are also important. In the first moment, the Bible can provide the stimulation and encouragement to engage in a particular kind of practice, in other words, reflection on scripture can give direction to our action. In the second moment, when we are in the midst of practical engagement, the Bible can provide a justifying and explaining role. In other words, scripture can help us understand what we are doing and help us adjust our practice as we go along, and also help us explain ourselves to others. In the third moment, after action has taken place, reflection on scripture can help us learn from what has happened. When we review our practice, particular biblical passages may resonate and help us to come to terms with any supposed 'failure' or deal with any supposed 'success', and help us to learn from the experience for what we can be done in the future.

The Bible and practice are in a dynamic relationship or conversation.[28] It is a lively interaction. It is clear that there can be no formula or strict logical framework between them. In theological terms, this is an arena for the work of God's Spirit. Nevertheless, as people take both their context and the scriptures seriously connections happen, people discover resonances that surprise and even shock them (see Alison Geary and Keith Lackenby, above), and because of their reading of part of the Bible find themselves engaging in new practice which can affect a town (see Michael Woods, above) or a major company (see Trevor Lockwood, above), breaking down barriers (see Alan Middleton and Stephen Owens, above) and enabling fellow Christians to carry on in a difficult and demanding world (see Alison Geary and Stephen Smyth, above).

The bible does not so much tell us what to do as inspire, provoke, and suggest. Current realities have to be taken seriously in all their uniqueness and difference from those of the Bible. Nevertheless, a conversation can take place between the Bible and us. As in any true conversation, both parties have things to say. To enact such a conversation entails speaking both for the Bible and for the contemporary situation, listening to both and allowing them to challenge each other. In other words, we become (as an individual or a group) a locus for such a conversation. It is unhelpful to have a one-sided conversation where only the Bible speaks or only the current situation.

Although it is dangerous (spiritually and practically) to equate Bible with practice, as if we can just read off its pages what to do, it is at least as dangerous to separate Bible and practice, as if they have nothing to do with each other. We must not give up the task of relating them to each other, and enabling them to speak to each other so that connections are made and practice, informed by the Bible, happens.

---

[1] Situation Analysis. Sheffield: Urban Theology Unit. See editions by John Vincent (1973), Christine Dodd (1991) and Ian Duffield (1998)

[2] John J. Vincent, 'Imaginative Identification', Epworth Review, 23.3, September 1996, pp. 14-20

[3] Clodovis Boff, Theology and Praxis: Epistemological Foundations. Maryknoll, NY: Orbis Books, 1987, pp. 145-6.

[4] Walter Wink, Transforming Bible Study. 1st edn. London: SCM Press, 1981; 2nd edn. London: Mowbray, 1990.

[5] See Robert McAfee Brown, Unexpected News: Reading the Bible with Third World Eyes. Philadelphia: Westminster Press, 1984, pp.15-16.

[6] Jorge Pixley, God's Kingdom. London: SCM Press, 1981, p.20.

[7] Stephen Smyth, Supporting Teachers in Catholic Schools. (2000), Ch.5B; Stephen Owens, Through the Green Fence: Showmen and Church in Dudley Wood (2001), Ch.6. See footnote 8.

[8] All these are unpublished MMin theses which are kept in the libraries at the Urban Theology Unit and Sheffield University.

[9] Michael Woods, Unblinkered Vision: A New Self-Image for the Future of Great Yarmouth (1998).

[10] Ibid., p.1.

[11] Ibid

[12] Alan Middleton, All Change for All Saints' (1999).

[13] Ibid., p.i.

[14] Ibid., p.95.

[15] Ibid., p.107.

[16] Trevor Lockwood, The Tension Between the Pastoral and Prophetic Roles of an Industrial Chaplain: Conflicting Roles in Industrial Mission (2000).

[17] Ibid., p.80.

[18] Ibid., p.i.

[19] Alison Geary, Purpose, Transition and Integrity: Middle-Class Methodists Looking for Meaning (1999).

[20] Ibid., p.i.

[21] Ibid., p.30.

[22] Ibid., p.220.

[23] Ibid., p.i.

[24] Keith Lackenby, From Old Chapels to New Church (1993).

[25] Ibid., p.100.

[26] Ibid., p.94.

[27] Ibid., p.i.

Andrew Davey

TOWARD AN URBAN HERMENEUTICS

1. Reclaiming a Canon

One of the most compelling pieces of television I have watched in recent years was Michael Bogdanov's 'Shakespeare on the Estate'.[1] The account of three weeks spent on an inner estate in Birmingham introducing the residents to the language, stories and characters of Shakespeare's plays.

The experiment produced a quite extraordinary interest and outpouring of creativity. Shakespeare was discussed and rehearsed in flats, drop-in centres, pubs and outside on the grass, among the type of people who would have stood in the Pit at The Globe and The Rose theatres. Parallels were drawn between Shakespearean characters and the experiences of the Ladywood community. Drugs, jealousy and fights were found in *Midsummer Nights Dream*, the anguish of a deserted woman was recognised in the experience of Lady Macduff, the experience of racial exclusion hit home in the *Merchant of Venice*, the anger of a family row in *Romeo and Juliet*, even the humour of the pub transvestites who offered their own version of the French lesson from *Henry V*.

Over the three weeks wide-spread suspicion was broken down and the warmth of the community asserted itself. The resulting scenes were a fascinating insight into how marginalised people in estate communities can take on a challenge with quite extraordinary outcomes. At the end of the programme Bogdanov reflected on the project:

> This has been an exhilarating experience but I feel angry and upset that there are communities all over the country, like Ladywood, full of talent and intelligence but wasted...

77

He goes onto recall the words of the slave Caliban to his master Prospero in *The Tempest*:

> You taught me language, and my profit on't
> Is, I know how to curse. [2]

Those of us who work alongside or within estate communities will have recognised many characters from Ladywood -the suspicious youth, the cynical observer outside the pub, the animated women's group, even the independent evangelical church - slightly out of synch. with the culture of the drop-in centres and pubs.

I suspect we would also recognise some of the barriers that were crossed in the course of the programme: the lack of self esteem and confidence; the resentment and suspicion of outsiders (particularly educated, white males); a sometimes all too accurate understanding of power in new relationships. Yet there was a willingness to give it a go, once they knew someone took them seriously. Here was something they wanted to do. 'We can do it.' 'I'm not just playing a tree you know.'

A different type of struggle was apparent as people came to terms with language predating the King James Bible. Some stuck with it, others went for a rewrite. At one point a participant challenged the language with its 'thee's and 'thou's- 'Why has it all been kept in - its not the Bible!'

Those of us working from a church base may wonder what the possibility of such a project using biblical material might be - what would people encounter given a clean slate? Even Bogdanov refused to believe that this was the participants first experience of Shakespeare.

> Ladywood is five minutes walk from the Birmingham Rep. And all those taking part had been to schools where the study of Shakespeare was compulsory, yet our brief rehearsal period seemed to be the first encounter with any of the language, stories or characters.

I expect the same could be said about their experience of the Christian story.

I am all too wary of the danger of romanticising a well edited television programme but the programme presented an authentic image of a marginalised community failed and alienated by an education system created

78

by those with no interest in seeing people from estate communities take control of there own lives let alone the cultural agenda. But within that community the project involving interaction with a canon of four hundred year old texts enabled a sizeable group to build their confidence and self esteem in a quite significant way. The project gave a glimpse of a citadel stormed and a canon reclaimed. The alienation of the working class from the cultural curriculum is an all too familiar story.

2. Encounter and interaction

The problem with any approach to scripture is overcoming its weirdness, the strangeness of its context, thought world and literary type. It is not just apparently an historical leap that needs to be made but also one of ideas and language. Some of the obstacles created by a hegemony of scholarship and other interest groups which have controlled the way in which the text is encountered and interpreted also need to be overcome.

In Britain this can be seen in the medieval attempts to dictate the language in which the text was available. As the Bible became available in the vernacular people began to read outside the traditional models of reading. Christopher Hill comments:

> The printed vernacular Bible was an important literary discovery, especially to those who learned to read via the scriptures. There are good stories in the Bible as well as models of conduct good and bad. We take knowledge of the Biblical myths for granted now: they have been absorbed into our culture - and are now being forgotten... The Bible was no longer the sacred text of the educated elite. [3]

The Levellers, Diggers and early Quakers all provided examples of alternative communities based on scripture put into action. One of the Digger leaders, Gerrard Winstanley, spoke of scripture being 'really and materially fulfilled' in the life of the believer.[4] The way in which the Bible has been treated in education over the following centuries is maybe an indication of the threat and power that the educated elite construed in the uncontrolled access to scripture. If a text is made remote, inaccessible or just plain weird readers will not realize its life changing, power threatening potential. Bogdanov's lament about Shakespeare is all too familiar. The maxim 'People tend to find in the Bible what they have been taught to find there' [5] is hardly applicable if there are no expectations of any significance.

Unfamiliarity with scripture is increasingly apparent among British Christians. Anglicans I suspect have been assisted by the disembodied use of scripture in their lectionary which gives makes little sense in terms of continuity/narrative. The application of scripture has tended to be reserved for individual devotion through Bible study notes. There is a need to rediscover the corporate approach to encountering scripture. People do have some of the tools - I know from experience that the 'hermeneutic of suspicion' is alive and well in south London. (I can remember deep suspicion of the New English Bible rendering of the first beatitude as 'Blessed are those who know their need of God' – the congreation were adamnt that it was the poor who were blessed – and the rich who were rewriting scripture). But it is not only about having tools but about the willingness to take part, to be challenged, to enact the vision that has been encountered.

3. New strategies

Despite the unfamilarliarity, I discovered in south London the inherent feeling that scripture was important. People wanted to repossess part of their tradition. The continuity and tradition about using scripture cannot be dismissed. We are not blowing the dust off a recently discovered collection of ancient texts but stepping into a legacy of encounter and interaction.

While working on a Bible Study programme for an inner London congregation I was particularly challenged by reading a collection of studies entitled *Stony the Road We Trod*[6], the work of a group of African American Bible scholars who have called into question the dominant western modes of biblical scholarship. These essays affirm the tradition of reading scripture within the black community, placing the front-line of interpretation within the churches, not the universities. They look for new approaches through which contemporary issues and experience can be addressed - not least the struggles of black women. The writers also examine the attitudes to race within the Bible and the racist assumptions of academic scholarship, asking why have the blacks and Africans of scripture and the ancient world been ignored, marginalised or whitened. Cain Hope Felder writes:

> We do not begin as if black people have just started reading the Bible. There is already a tradition. What can we learn from your grandfather and my aunt about what the Bible means?

> We need to avoid a "trickle-down" theory of interpretation, in which the scholar gives and the people eventually receive. There has to be real, on-going interaction. The experience of

the black church has given to some kinds of sources - sermons, call narratives, the spirituals - an authority almost on a par with the biblical canon. What does this say about the Bible as a way of communicating? Are there patterns in the kinds of things that are joined together? Over and over again, the message is clear: What happened long ago is my story - my Lord delivered Daniel, why not me? [7]

Felder and his colleagues point to new ways of understanding how we read the Bible. Particularly in the light of the African American experience. The Christian community is where that process begins as people tell their own and their community's story in the light of scripture.

This approach put the emphasis on the community seeking to establish its identity and its mission through its interaction with scripture. Analysing the way and the context in which the Bible is encountered is a concern which be discerned progressing from recent movements of literary criticism.

Narrative criticism looks to the stories or texts as we have them in their final form. Those who created this final form were not solely consolidators or collectors but skilled storytellers concerned with the 'internal organisation of its story world' [8]The Abraham narrative as we have it in Genesis is read by the majority of readers as a whole with little need for source or documentary theories. In the act of reading the reader encounters a plot: events, characters and setting. The reader also encounters a text completed with certain expectations. No incident in a narrative can be seen in isolation as each is part of the editor's discourse. To understand the intentions of the final editor (or story teller) of Genesis concerning Israel's understanding of itself, the communities around it and its destiny is an important task for the reader and critic. Brueggemann sees their stories as a vital inheritance in the community of faith:

> The stories do not exist by themselves nor for themselves. They exist as they are told and valued, transmitted and remembered by a community which is seriously engaged in a life of ministry and faith. [9]

Narrative theology is a parallel movement to that of narrative criticism concerned with the place of individual and corporate stories in the Christian community. Narrative within the Christian faith goes beyond the scriptural narrative into the individual Christian's self-understanding and that of the church. This is manifest in its rituals, creeds, histories and other activities.

There is an essential narrative quality in the human experience, as the present is interpreted by memory and moulded by the anticipation of the future. As the Christian narrative interacts with the individual's story a new synthesis, a new consciousness is possible for the individual and the faith community in which it is shared.

In a multicultural congregation the biblical narratives have an increasing importance as we attempt to affirm what we have in common alongside our individual stories. Narrative theology affirms the psychological need of human beings to be aware of and to be able to relate one's own story. The biblical narratives provide a common memory for the Christian community which provides the markers for basis of self-understanding here and now. Doctrines and revelation are part of a narrative which Christians recall and continue to participate in. George W. Stroup defines a community as

> ...a group of people who have come to share a common past, who understand particular events in the past to be of decisive importance for interpreting the present, who anticipate the future by means of a shared hope, and who express their identity in a common narrative. [10]

> To live in the Christian community and to participate in its common life is to share a commitment that its traditions and its narratives are more appropriate than those of other communities and other traditions for making decisions and interpreting the world. [11]

This is not to discard the diversity within the Christian community. The tradition is made up of many narratives, moulded by the new situations in which that community finds itself. The diversity of cultures and backgrounds in a multi-ethnic congregation, therefore, sends us back to dialogue with tradition to discover our emergent identity. It is against such a background of constant that many congregations struggle to be faithful and sustainable communities. When studying the story of Abraham such a group discovered an individual story which also involved a community living against and within a number of cultures (Chaldean, Cannanite, Egyptian) and their values. Certainly a paradigm of a community living in a time of seemingly global transition. Those within the Abrahamic community had roots elsewhere yet they were marked out by their practice of community life in sharing blessings, welcoming strangers, hoping for something better against all odds, and passing on its traditions and beliefs in its future. This 'memory' is as vital to the heterogeneous groups which made up the early Israelite confederation as it is to the self-understanding of marginalised urban people who were an integral part of the first Christian communities of the New Testament.

Reading has come to be understood in itself as an experience that requires analysis. The reader approaches the text with his or her own story, and places that alongside the text being encountering. Interpretation takes place during the dynamic act of reading [12]and when the reader looks back once the text is completed. **Reader-response criticism** covers a variety of approaches which attempt to understand the processes going on as stories were read in their original setting and are re-read in each new situation by individuals and by 'interpretative communities'. To understand the socio-economic settings of the author's communities gives us insights into their intentions, within the text there are clues concerning those they were writing for - 'the implied reader'. The communities which handle the texts change with each generation. There is talk of the reader 'activating' the text, unleashing implicit meaning. As the text is encountered in each new time or place a new 'reading' is possible, as previous memories meet new actions and insights. It is this which can lead to the old hegemonies being challenged and broken. One needs to be aware of the strategy by which one is reading. This is particularly apparent in how the reader deals with what is not in the text ('filling the gaps') an exercise which may come all too easily when encountering an incident related by three (or four) apparently similar gospels.

Felder and colleagues consider the community of which they are part to have an important and unique tradition when it comes to the use of the Biblical text. For example, African American readers will react and interpret texts concerning servanthood and slavery in a particular way. Similarly women in that community will read under the double experience of being marginalised as a woman as well as being black:

> The strategies one employs in reading a text will depend in
> large part upon what one's overall disposition is toward the act
> of reading. (...) Texts are read not only within contexts; a text's
> meaning is also dependent on the pretext(s) of its readers. [13]

Urban Christians I have worked with have brought with them a wide range of educational experience and reading ability. They brought with them experiences which were personal but also the experience of attempting to read (or listen to) the scripture as a community which considers the text to be significant in the latter part of the twentieth century in inner London. The black experience and community in Britain has a different story to that we hear from the Americas. Felder's colleagues readings come mostly from within the historic black-led churches with their roots in emancipation and segregation. Despite this it was interesting that group picked up on the incidents considered vital by African American women, such as those concerning Hagar when we were looking at the Abraham stories. The experience of race was one element in our studies which also embraced stories of migration, rootlessness and being at the margins of a society, of attempting to live in heterogeneous communities both secular and sacred.

Regardless of attempts to read the Bible free of certain presuppositions we needed to be aware that our studies still took place from within an historic Christian tradition with a chequered history concerning its treatment of those from outside its customary constituency. The seventeenth century readers mentioned earlier found that they could no longer consider themselves to be part of 'catholic' Christianity. Our Bible studies reminded us of the tension between the catholic and the local incarnations of the church as attempts are made to live in a national church where the disparity of wealth is increasingly obvious, along with the assumption from some quarters that catholic equals uniformity in matters of mission, practice and biblical interpretation.

4. Striving for Community Identity

We began with a secular example of a drama project in an urban community. *The Art of Regeneration* [14] is a recent report from the Joseph Rowntree Foundation. Subtitled: *urban renewal thorough cultural activity* the report explores the underlying characteristics and issues raised by 100 arts projects - festivals, carnivals, community plays etc. Like Bogdaov's project these initiatives are considered to make a positive and often unique contribution to local vitality and through that to local urban renewal. The following reasons are offered:

- They engage people's creativity, and so lead to problem solving.
- They are about meanings, and enable dialogue between people and social groups.
- They encourage questioning, and the imaging of possible futures.
- They offer self-expression, which is an essential characteristic of the active citizen.
- They are unpredictable and, exciting and fun. [15]

I think this links in with the experience of many urban Christians as well as the developing notion of performance in narrative theology. During my time as a parish priest in Peckham, South East London, the most memorable liturgical exercise of the year was without the doubt the Good Friday Stations of the Cross. In some aspects a very traditional act of catholic piety but one of the few liturgical services of the year that encouraged a real embodiment of the Christian story, through movement and narrative. The event took place in a bare church, occasionally spilling out into the car park, as people followed Christ's journey. Although the church space was familiar the atmosphere of the service was very different. The church had been stripped on Maundy Thursday, the procession took us all to parts of the building, and outside which were not regularly used.. At the end we gathered under a plain suspended cross, often with tears, sometimes barely hoping that there would be good news on Easter Day. For a moment a glimpse had been caught of a divine moment. Urban churches which take drama onto the street during Passiontide report similar experiences.

A liturgy which enables the process of embodiment is an enriching experience for all concerned. How I want to ask can such embodiment happen in all our encounters with scripture. In another context, Bishop Lesslie Newbigin, writes of 'The congregation as Hermeneutic of the Gospel'[16] Our experience of the gospel should be evident through its embodiment in the public life of the church. This is the praxis of the liberation theologians and the dynamics of performance described by narrative theology:

> In Christian Theology I see three dynamics of performance in line with the content and middle distance realism of the gospel story in its Old Tesament and New Testament context. The first is that of active relationship with god most explicit in worship. The second is that of life together in a community of faith and love. The third is that of prophetic speech and action in witness, evangelism and dedication to peace, justice and goodness.[17]

5. Context, Creativity and Connectivity

It is with such expectations that I want to spend the final part of this paper looking at the basis for a urban hermeneutics. If the canon is to be reclaimed those responsible for the formation of urban congregations need to put fresh emphasis on context, creativity and connectivity. Hermeneutics needs to understood as a significant event and as an enterprise which encompasses the total life of the church - local and catholic.

Context
The social location of theological reflection is increasingly recognised as an important factor in the theory and practise of Christian discipleship,

particularly strategies for biblical interpretation. Urban congregations need to overcome dislocated attitude to scripture - there is often a failure to make connections or identify with the biblical narrative. If the process is to start with those who have been failed by the education system then the participants lack of confidence in written culture needs to recognised. Familiarity with the text ranges from traditional acquaintance to misunderstanding and ignorance. Strategies need to be considered by which the Bible is accessible to the marginalised as a tool for faith and action. This is also true for patterns of ministry.

Social location might be considered a fact of life[18] - the total of the influences, pressures, experiences that shape the lives of individuals and communities with direct bearing on the interpretation reached, but social location needs to be made explicit. How our situation affect the way we approach the text? What pressures are we under from others to read as if things were otherwise? What dominant readings need to be rejected because we know the world to be different? How will our encounter with scripture affect the way we understand our situation?

Context is where the encounter will take place, from where we will be challenged and from where connections need to be made with those who are seeking new possibility. The social location will also include the community in which the reading takes place.

Community

The Communities which grapple with the scriptures are described variously as 'interpretative communities', 'receiving communities' and 'listening communities'. This grappling should lead those communities to define themselves through their communal and individual decisions and actions, that is their ethics.

What are the assumptions and expectations of a community approaching scripture? As we have already seen contemporary urban Christians are not the first to embark on this enterprise. Even with an acknowledged break in the continuity and attempts, conscience or otherwise, to stop the *plebs* getting at the Bible, we approach scripture expecting to get something from it. The Bible has a significance in the church because it is a canonical community. Interacting with scripture is a faith exercise, as the community seeks meaning in its own context globally, historically, culturally and asks what does God ask of us, here and now? The imagination of faith refuses to be content with human arrangements – social, economic, political, urban, rural, which are not based on the practice of human freedom in the presence of God. That imagination will pertinently challenge those arrangements through envisioning alternatives, through prophetic speech and action, through the creation of communities that include, strengthen and give integrity to those at the margins.

[1] Shakespeare on the Estate with Michael Bogdanov, directed by Penny Woolcock BBC Bristol 1994

[2] The Tempest 1:2, line 362

[3] Christopher Hill, The English Bible and the Seventeenth Century Revolution. Harmondsworth: Allen Lane/Penguin, 1993, p.39.

[4] Paul M. Siegal, The Meek and the Militant. London: Zed Press, 1986, p. 94.

[5] Robert M. Fowler, 'Reader Response Criticism: Figuring Mark's Reader' in Janice Capel Anderson and Stephen D. Moore, eds., Mark and Method - New Approaches in Biblical Studies. Minneapolis: Fortress Press, 1992, p. 53.

[6] Cain Hope Felder, ed., Stony the Road We Trod: African American Biblical Interpretation. Minneapolis: Fortress Press, 1991.

[7] Ibid. p.9.

[8] Janice Capel Anderson and Stephen D. Moore, 'Introduction: The Lives of Mark' in Janice Capel Anderson and Stephen D. Moore, eds., Mark and Method - New Approaches in Biblical Studies. Minneapolis: Fortress Press, 1992, p. 12..

[9] Walter Brueggemann, Genesis. JKP: Richmond, 1982, p.4.

[10] George W. Stroup, The Promise of Narrative Theology. London: SCM Press, 1984, p.133.

[11] Ibid. p.167.

[12] Wolfgang Iser suggests the reader goes through the experience of struggle : 'We look forward, we look back, we decide, we change our decisions, we form expectations, we are shocked by their nonfulfilment, we question, we muse, we accept we reject' quoted by Robert M. Fowler, 'Reader Response Criticism: Figuring Mark's Reader' in Janice Capel Anderson and Stephen D. Moore, eds., Mark and Method - New Approaches in Biblical Studies. Minneapolis: Fortress Press, 1992, p.58.

[13] Renita J Weems, 'Reading Her Way through the Struggle', in Cain Hope Felder, ed., Stony the Road We Trod: African American Biblical Interpretation. Minneapolis: Fortress Press, 1991, p.62.

[14] Landry, Charles; Greene, Lesley; Matarasso, Francois & Bianchini, Franco, The Art of Regeneration: Urban renewal through cultural activity. Stroud: Comedia, 1996. Summary - Social Policy Summary 8 March 1996, York: Joseph Rowntree Foundation, 1996.

[15] Summary ibid. p.4

[16] Lesslie Newbigin, Gospel in a Pluralist Society. SPCK: London, 1989, p.222.

[17] David Ford, 'System, Story, Performance', in Stanley Hauerwas & L. Gregory Jones, Why Narrative? Readings in Narrative Theology. Eerdmans: Grand Rapids, 1989, p.203.

[18] See Okure, Teresa 'Reading from This Place ; Some Problems and Perspectives' in Segovia, Fernando F. & Tolbert, Mary Ann, eds., Reading from this Place- Volume 2: Social Location and Biblical Interpretation in Global Perspective. Minneapolis: Fortress Press, 1995

Ann Weatherley

FAILURE – IN BIBLE AND IN LIFE

1. Days Like These

The phone is ringing; the phone is ringing! Rushed out of my blissful sleep I scamper down the stairs. Don't know the time but it's definitely early as the rooks are beginning their daily arguments about housing rights. It's Bet on the blower. "Jasper's got out again. Can you find him for me?" Bet is in her eighties and full of life and spirit and even with a dodgy hip and walking frame will take on the world and his wife, but neither she nor her husband, Stan, can catch their energetic dog. Jasper alas has no road sense. I chuck on some clothes, negotiate the crazy speeding traffic on the main road to ask the local mechanic to look for him. I search his usual haunts, but he is not to be found. "He's rabbiting again". Stan, now bed-bound with terminal cancer, is having breakfast. I tell Bet for the umpteenth time not to worry about getting me out. Later, Jasper, looking pleased with himself, makes a grand entrance in my back garden!

Bleary-eyed, I stagger home still tired after a night of coughing from asthma, and go back to bed. I'm woken by Pete's sobbing voice on the answer phone. Can't understand much but he's in a state. Something about his violent wife and his children. I'll get the full story later. It's 7.30 and I snooze for an hour only to be woken by Sue's voice. She needs to get to the DSS by 10 so I get to cuddle her 3 month old daughter Anna, who is gorgeous and makes me feel broody. With Anna laying on my chest we both have a snooze. Sue returns and over a cuppa she tells me about her battle with the Social.

Stella phones and is up the creek. The Church has reminded her again that she's black, a woman and a mere appendage to her husband. She feels isolated, hurt and bruised. She's had a lifetime of abuse meted out by manipulative Christian leaders and her confidence is easily crushed. Mel is wise, beautiful both inside and out, and has a sensational singing voice. I listen to her fears knowing that she needs to talk the worry out and hear some words of love, encouragement and belief.

Cathi pops in for lunch and a bit of TLC. She's struggling to complete her course work   at college - her way of keeping herself together. Years of emotional and physical abuse by her husband resulted in her cutting her wrists, being sectioned and losing her daughters and home. The abuser continues his abusive ways with their children thanks to the institutions who don't seem to be able to see the wood for the trees. No-one listens. Cathi's written off as a hysterical nutcase. Cathi needs to talk it out and then goes back to college.

It's now 2 pm and Pete arrives. He married the wrong person for the wrong reasons. Tender-hearted, caring and compassionate with a severe lack of confidence - a legacy of childhood neglect.   Seen as a bright star at theological college, he married someone he felt he could help, encourage and give a better life. In return she shattered his fragile confidence with emotional abuse in the day and physical abuse in the middle of the night. Forced to leave the ministry he loved, and rejected by church hierarchy who didn't understand, he contemplated suicide. After seven years of talking out the pain he is coming to a place where he is beginning to learn who he really is and not what he has been manipulated into thinking he is.

Chris phones and the tentacles of his past tightly cling on in the guise of "vindictive and callous Tax Men" as the solicitor and CAB rep called them. Chris' honesty and integrity has not been rewarded and for the third time they are taking him to court. I offer to go with him and warn him that if Inland Revenue try to pull a fast one again (last time they lied to the Judge!) I'm likely to head-butt them! Every time Chris begins to get to a point where life is looking quite good, the Inland Revenue sneak up and savage him. I wouldn't mind but they spend more money taking Chris to court that what he owes them!

With a cup of tea I sit and ponder the day. It's not always so manic but the agony that folk go through seems to have grown over the years. Increasingly poor health reduces my ability to get around as well as I did 15 years ago, but I can still listen and make cups of tea and can still attempt a 'heart-centred hug'[1] . I think of Mandy and Dad and where all my feeble endeavours to be a good listener and a long-term carer began.

2. Dark Days

"I'll never see Leah grow up or see her happily married." I felt such sorrow for Mandy whose ravaged body was gradually being eaten away by cancer, but somehow I sensed a spiritual torture which was perhaps just as agonising. "I can talk to you because I know you understand pain". Mandy knew I'd been nursing my beloved father who was himself dying of cancer. Our shared grief brought about a deep, reciprocal love and respect. We spent hours sharing our lives and listening to Mandy's catalogue of abuse in the guise of loving criticism is enough to make your hair stand on end. The last time we shared together we cried for each other. A month later Mandy died and at her funeral I unashamedly wept whilst others danced around. As the coffin that held Mandy's tiny body went past her mother stopped and put her arms around me and said, "Thank you for caring about Mandy so much, she knew you really loved her".

Despite the grief I was experiencing - compounded by my uncle, my aunt and my friend's recent deaths' and my father's imminent death - I knew what God had been calling me to do; what he had always been calling me to do in this life. Despite our brief friendship the experience of knowing and caring for Mandy left an indelible imprint in my spirit of what being alongside those who suffer really means, and my life was never the same again. Although at the time I was doing what came naturally. As Mandy was so weak I used to prepare meals, play with her daughter, Leah, clean and polish and sometimes wash Mandy's hair.

Mandy's illness had engendered an obsessional "healing" fever in the church, that completely marginalised Mandy's inner agony and her need to talk about death and grief for the life she may not have. At 22 she was "too young too die" and only "faith in God's healing" would save her and "all those who don't have faith should leave the church" the pastor had said. As for my dad, well he'd had his " three score and ten". What more could one expect? The pastor however had no idea who my father was or what he had been to me in my life. Neither did he attempt to find out. Another church leader added "it's not as hard as losing a husband or wife or child, is it?" How would I know? I was neither married nor had any children. It all seemed so clinical and cold and bore no relation to people, their history or feelings. It all smacked of "I really don't want to be bothered with this" - far easier to be "joyful" about the possibility of healing than confront death and all that death raises in people's minds.

Later that week I told the pastor about my own studies on healing, saying that I did not believe God "plays dice with people's lives". Surely "God showed compassion by sending Jesus to redeem a lost world". The pastor, reputed to be a "gentle man", but looking at me angrily, said "Do you know what your trouble is? You love your father more than you love God and that is preventing you from hearing what God was saying to the Church". I was shattered. Then he said he wanted to pray for me! I retorted, "you're the last person I want to pray for me" and walked out.

It was the final straw in a long line of destructive comments made to me and about me that I had previously accepted from my 'betters', and that had left my confidence in tatters. Often I would feel the hurt of others and cry with those who cried, only to be met with the criticism "you are far too sensitive...pull yourself together". Such comments would often leave me drowning in the despair of failure.

I left the pastor's house with tears running down my face wondering how he could judge me so harshly when he had never kept one of his promises to visit my father. What did he know about my life or my father who had been such a kind, loving man and had sacrificed so much for me, his adopted daughter; about how he had brought me up single-handed after my alcoholic mother, who beat me to a pulp every day, had left in one of her drunken stupors; who had fought through the courts, battled with social workers, to keep me. What greater picture of a Christ-like love could any human being hope to find? This pastor who had never listened, had the temerity to make such an accusation. As my father's illness worsened it became impossible for me to attend services and meetings and the minister responded by withdrawing my name from membership as I "had obviously left the church".

When my father saw my distress he began to blame himself saying "it's all my fault, all this time you've been looking after me and it's been too much for you". I was horrified and reassured him that my anxiety was caused by someone's unkind words. How could I tell him the truth? Unconvinced, my father fretted terribly and I found it hard to forgive the pastor for bringing such pain into his final weeks of life. At that moment I decided never to go to that church again; a decision which was to bring immense relief and such peace during that last period my father and I shared. My father's health began to decline and for the last eight weeks he vomited all day and every day until he could no longer take in the smallest amounts of fluid. Gradually he slipped into a coma and died in my arms. Loyal and loving friends family gathered round and helped me to overcome my deep grief. For quite I wanted to be alone and in the quietness of my solitude all the pain from the past seemed to press in on me - 'In solitude I get rid of my scaffolding... naked, vulnerable, weak, sinful, deprived, broken- nothing'[2] .

3. Blessed are the broken pieces

Blessed are the broken pieces, for they shall not be swept under the carpet. Broken and shattered but determined to hang on, clinging to the love my father had given me, and grappling with what seemed revolutionary threads in my bible studies that kept me going. I read the Bible again and again, making copious notes and recognising themes and links between the narratives of Samuel, Kings, and Chronicles for instance, and placing all the Prophets within their historical context; linking up the Old Testament with the New. I began to see that this 'culture of success' I had encountered in my church was more often to do with Christians attempting to appear successful than any genuine evidence of spirituality and faith. It left many others who were struggling with the pain in their lives feeling marginalised as 'failures'; and it seemed far removed from the characters I had met in the Old Testament.

Moses emerged as one of the most wonderful 'failures'. Having spent forty years in Egypt thinking he was a 'success' a high-handed mistake resulted in Moses high-tailing it to the desert to spend forty years shuffling around a load of sheep and feeling a 'failure'. Down on his uppers, he is called by God to undertake a job that only he could do and what does Moses say? "O Lord, please send someone else to do it."[3] That's real; that's honesty; and I loved his integrity. At a similar point in his life, Jeremiah told God that he didn't know how to speak prophetic words because he was a mere child. And as for Jonah he ran off to Tarshish when God asked him to go to Nineveh.[4] I love the beauty and meaning of the Psalms but they became more real and alive because they showed David (and others) having a good old whinge when the going got tough. Then there is of course every mother's 'nightmare' child, Joseph. Not content with flaunting before his brothers his 'richly ornamented robe' - the gift of a doting father to a favourite son - Joseph also misuses his God-given talent for interpreting dreams to try to put his brothers in their place. We all know what happened to Joseph. Or do we?

4. The Son of Encouragement

All these men were not initially pillars of society; they didn't have the same upbringing; didn't come from the same section of society. One thing they did have in common however - they were all flawed. In all their different ways they had to struggle with themselves, and with God, so that they could learn to be alongside others. Some of them only knew the agony and cost of following

God; the abuse of those who refused to hear the truth; often resulting in their untimely and horrific executions. This period of study brought such comfort and joy because I realised for the first time that so-called 'failure' and 'lack of faith' went with the territory of attempting to do what God wanted and being faithful to his calling.

Alongside my studies I continued to read the Old Testament for the fourth time and the New Testament for the umpteenth time. But this time, when I came to Barnabas I seemed to be drawn into the heart of his story. Barnabas saw something in Paul that no-one else recognised. It was on his recommendation that Paul had been welcomed into the church. In the 'Son of Encouragement', I found someone who was not willing to go along with the 'crowd, but spoke up in support of the outcast Paul, despite the evidence. What did Barnabas see that convinced him of Paul's conversion from his murderous and conspiratorial past to a believer in Jesus? Did he see Paul through rose-tinted glasses?

It's very doubtful that today's church would welcome Paul with open arms given the evidence. It is all too easy to say 'of course we would trust him,' but that is because we know what happens later. Barnabas however didn't know the end of the story and yet he stood by Paul and supported him. But why? Surely it was because he saw in Paul a man who had once been hated, but now needed to be trusted so his life could be turned around. Not that Paul ever became perfect. One of the things I had to unlearn was the idea, so prevalent in much church teaching, that Paul became an untarnished super-apostle who could do and say no wrong. That is far from true as Barnabas himself was to discover Ð and Paul is a far more interesting and real because in one crucial episode of his ministry he not only failed, but had the grace at the end of his life to admit that Mark was not only a man to be trusted but one of the only people who did not desert him Paul at the end of his life.

Barnabas showed both courage and foresight in supporting Paul. Years later, when the argument between Barnabas and Paul[5] concerning John Mark erupted, Barnabas is again supportive but this time his support is given to John Mark. They were related of course but is this sufficient to explain why Barnabas felt able to trust his cousin? After all John Mark had a habit of "running away" didn't he? Barnabas saw something in him that was unique and valuable. Paul, however didn't want to know. He forgets the love and commitment he had the joy of receiving himself from Barnabas and utterly rejects Mark. He only looked at the evidence. John Mark was unreliable and a liability. Barnabas however stuck to his conviction that Mark could become, would become strong and trustworthy if only someone stood alongside him, helping him to overcome the fear that was dogging his life.

The 'disagreement' between Paul and Barnabas was no mere misunderstanding - the full impact of the Greek is not well expressed in English - but was a full-blown and fierce exchange after which the fruitful apostolic partnership was finally torn apart.

5. Childhood lasts forever

Jesus said 'Let the little children come to me, and do not hinder them, for the kingdom of God belongs to such as these'. There is something about the trusting and truthfulness of a little child that is so beautiful and God-like. Shattering and damaging a child's spirit through neglect, abuse and pain can have life-long consequences. My own experiences and those of many who have come to the house over the years seem to share pain and grief in childhood that affected them so deeply as they grew into adulthood.

Although I was born in the East End I lived all my formative years in one room in a North London house. Along with 4 other families, we all shared one toilet and one sink with cold water which stood outside our door. Community life centred around the market from where most people bought everything from vegetables to their socks! Although materially poor as a child, I like others was unaware of it because my life was no different to that of my neighbours. The sting of poverty was to become painfully obvious later when exposed to the material wealth of others.

Poverty became part and parcel of living in a community riddled with financial and educational inequality but my plight was compounded by my mother's destructive alcoholism. By the time I reached the age of three my mother's drink problem had caused two evictions as she drank away the rent. My father later told me how he had once come home from work to discover my mother and me missing and all his belongings on the street. We were finally reduced to living in the one-roomed home I remember most. Mother was essentially a kind-hearted woman who would always ensure that I was cared for whilst she went on her drinking binges. However most memories are filled with the seemingly endless times she came home in the early hours of the morning shouting and screaming at my father whilst dragging me out of bed, and the beatings I received from her during the day. I would often hide in the wardrobe, with my favourite teddy bear for comfort, to escape her angry tirades.

My childhood fear lead to bed-wetting. This problem was made worse by our G.P. who concluded that as he could find nothing physically wrong I must therefore be "lazy". Despite tearfully remonstrating with my parents and the doctor that it always happened in my sleep, no-one listened. What the doctor said had to be true. Bed wetting always happened during the nights when my mother came home in one of her drunken stupors. The doctor's ill-informed diagnosis however led to five years of physical abuse and an almost paralysing fear of my mother's retribution at any sign of my 'problem'. It was however the inevitability of being punished rather than the punishment itself that left me screaming and hiding in fear.

My mother's alcoholism also led her into prostitution to support her habit. Childhood memories are filled with shadowy images of pubs, the smell of alcohol and different men all called "uncle". My mother's alcoholic intoxication reached a climax resulting in a fight and my mother's final departure. It was to be another three or four years before I saw my mother again when she sued my father for physical abuse - a ruse to gain money.

At the court I sat between my father and my aunt and when my mother appeared I pretended not to recognise her because my child-like understanding saw her appearance as a threatening force to the peace and love I had with my father. My lie haunted me for years. My mother's face and neck were covered in bandages but there was no mistaking her wild red hair - the essence of my childhood nightmares. As everybody went into the court I was left completely alone. The fear of this moment has never left me. Many times after this incident I would tearfully prayed to God that I would die before my father because I couldn't deal with the fear of being left alone ever again. I would be reduced to tears on the days when my father came home late from work, believing that like my mother, my father had left me because I had been naughty.

Despite visits and threats from social workers that I should be taken into 'care' I was eventually allowed to stay with my father - a real miracle! The many good memories of times my father and I spent together were marred by experiences of my formative years which left indelible scars on my life. I had to revisit them again and again as I struggled to come to terms with the past.

What had John Mark experienced I wondered? Had his childhood been similar? Had his confidence been so undermined that it led to his 'desertions'. If his childhood experiences were negative then perhaps his actions of 'desertion' would not be surprising. According to most commentators there

95

were about ten years between Barnabas leaving Paul and taking John Mark to Jerusalem, and Paul asking for John Mark to be brought to him for the 'comfort' that only John Mark could bring. Barnabas, encourager, supporter, 'paraclete' was loving, committed and had the wisdom to know John Mark needed a father-figure to help bring out those hidden and suppressed qualities he undoubtedly had. We know they met because Peter talks about his 'son' referring to John Mark.

> Walk gently, then, with your frailty, allow it to bless you.
> It will not cripple you unless you run from it.
> Embrace it instead. Carry it as one carries
> the cherished secret of great wealth hidden away
> in a holy, eternal space, like a treasure hidden in a field... [6]

For me too learning to live a new life meant facing past agonies, pain and trauma just as John Mark had, with people who would be alongside and help me walk with the pain without being crushed by it.

> 'I want to unfold; I don't want to stay folded anywhere
> because where I am folded there I am a lie'.
> Rainer Maria Rilke

This new period would not be a time of 'contemplating my own navel' but learning rich lessons from God in the 'desert' place. Lonely but not alone, laying bare the agony and pain but also drinking in new life. Moses spent many years in the desert being prepared for the work ahead. Paul spent three years in the Arabian desert before he went up to Jerusalem to meet Peter. Joseph spent time in a pit and in prison and when the dream of his brothers bowing down before him was finally realised, Joseph had to turn way with tears in his eyes as he recognised the folly of his youth. The place of preparation and understanding and working through their pain was located in 'desert places'.

6. The Way of the Desert

Far from being a forbidding place my desert, my solitude became a source of great comfort and where I found new people and new life. My 'Barnabas' friends such as Michael Eastman[7] introduced me to the Boff brothers *Introduction to Liberation Theology*[8], Jim Punton's *Messiah Papers*[9] and Roger Dowley's *Lost Bequest*.[10] These books became very important and opened a treasure chest before me. Dowley and Punton's comments on Hebrew words were particularly important.

yasha[11] -'to bring into a spacious uncramped environment...being at one's ease, free to develop without hindrance...to liberate from what is narrow and oppressive' totally liberated me. Just like when 'children run free in wide open places or when people from the towns and cities respond to the openness of the countryside or seeing the expansiveness of the sea'

What a wonderful picture of God's saving grace . So then 'salvation not only describes the release from that which threatens, hinders or oppresses but must also be a release into that which brings freedom, well-being and wholeness'. Salvation no longer remained a once-in-a-lifetime event nor was it static. Salvation was a living journey that took you from oppression to life in all its abundance. This picture was further enhanced by the Hebrew 'Shalom' - so often misunderstood due to its narrow interpretation as 'peace'. Punton says:

'Shalom' is the flowering fruit of salvation yasha where the English translation of peace is not profound enough to bring out its full emphasis. .... Shalom is a state where things are balanced out...a term describing the relationship between man and man, or man and the community, or even between man and God. Shalom is not so much an attitude of inward peace as an external well-being; it is a dynamic entity rather than a static condition.'

These new readings filled me with new life and inner peace, giving me confidence to know that the call to care for others and be alongside those in need was indeed from God. All the pain, abuse and rejection seemed to have had some purpose after all, giving me insight, understanding and a sensitivity to other people's needs. In turn those in need recognised something that allowed them to trust me, knowing that I would never leave or desert them.

'One learns of the pain of others by suffering one's own pain, by turning inside oneself; By finding one's own soul. It is important to know of pain.It destroys our self-pride, our arrogance, our indifference to others'. Chaim Potok

John Mark had been seen as a 'deserter', rejected by Paul and yet after being cared for by people who came alongside he became much treasured by those with whom he shared his life, not least by Paul himself. In Philemon 24 John Mark is mentioned as being with Paul as a 'fellow-worker'; in Colossians 4 John Mark is a 'fellow-prisoner' who Paul says is to be 'welcomed if he comes to you'; in 2 Timothy Paul, in prison alone and deserted asks for John Mark to be brought to him.

Here at the end of Paul's life when he is living under the shadow of execution, it is Mark that Paul asks for because he is a 'comforter'. The English translation does not bring out the true depth of who Mark had become. The Greek for 'helper' for instance is one who brings assistance, especially to the weak and needy. A 'fellow-helper' is one who is 'at hand', 'standing with', a 'labourer' and a 'companion' a 'paraclete' another Barnabas. Mark the 'comforter' and 'consolation' corresponds to the name "Menahem" given by the Hebrews to the Messiah. The 'comfort' Mark brought to Paul is like the application of soothing oil to a painful, recurring sore that the recipient cannot apply to his own wound.

7. Digging Deep

In my own painful experience, I moved from a paralysing fear and insecurity to a place of peace. Understanding the roots of my fear finally released me from them. The thought of facing the fear is often much harder than the fear itself. As I dug deep into my own being I found a well from which I could drink and from which others could also find refreshment. Being alongside people became an active, participatory process; a living, developing concept not a 'quick-fix' solution. My own gut reactions had been right; folk needed non-judgemental acceptance, space, peace and importantly time; time to talk, to cry, to sleep, to shout, to scream out their pain and anguish. For some, their pain had been shut up in their heads and in their beings for so long that it took months and sometimes years for them to fully express all the horrors; bit by bit, piece by piece. They needed time to discover a place where they could live with their past without being crushed by its pain; a place where they would be free to develop all those hidden treasures locked away inside.

As I began to 'walk' with others they too walked with me and relationships were formed Of course I had my critics. One person informed me that I was "backsliding" and moving away from God's rules concerning discipleship and that by fraternising with lame ducks my spiritual life was being harmed. And after all "if people can't sort themselves out then I should leave them to get on with it". By this time I couldn't care less what people said. I was convinced that long-term commitment was the right path for me to follow. I realised, of course, that my scriptural understanding was as open to criticism from my inquisitors as I myself questioned their interpretations. People had been "saved" and "miraculously healed" by their ministry whereas I had no such proof. But my life had changed because people had stood alongside me through the dark days. It was the love and compassion shared during those times that put flesh on the bones of God's word. Jesus was the word and really did dwell among us and so the word became 'flesh', is 'flesh', will always be 'flesh' through his fellow-workers.

I am not a professionally trained counsellor or pastor, but God gave me the ability and patience to listen and be alongside those who feel alone and desperate. I do not clock watch about how long it takes for people to work through their pain and come into a peaceful and creative place. When people come to the house I give them my undivided attention as I do to those who phone. God has given me peace about offering long-term, open-ended commitment, and I have had the joy of seeing people develop and begin to open up like flowers in the springtime to all that life has to offer them. I continue to listen and learn so that I may truly become that 'comforter' and 'encourager', God's person, continually aware of the pain of being human and failing but nevertheless believing that God chooses to work with imperfect, struggling people, even someone like me.[12]

---

[1] Kathleen Keating, The Little Book of Hugs: "The heart-centred hug is full and lingering, caring and tender, open and genuine, supportive and strong". Angus & Robertson Publishers, 1998

[2] Henri J.M. Nouwen, The Way of the Heart. DLT, 1981 p. 27

[3] Exodus 4:13

[4] Jonah 1:1-3

[5] Acts 15:39

[6] Macrina Wiedenkehr, A Tree Full of Angels. HarperSan Franciso, 1990. p. 23

[7] Michael Eastman is General Secretary of Evangelical Coalition for Urban Mission and formerly C.E.O of Frontier Youth Trust.

[8] Leonardo and Clodovis Boff, Introducing Liberation Theology. Burns & Oates, 1987

[9] Jim Punton, The Messiah Papers. Frontier Youth Trust

[10] Roger Dowley, Towards the Recovery of a Lost Bequest. E.C.U.M, 1980.

[11] Yasha is first mentioned in Exodus 14:30 when Moses leads the Israelites from slavery to freedom.

[12] With heartfelt thanks to my ever supportive and loving family and many friends along the way who stuck with me through good and bad times, and to all who gave me permission to use their stories. Special thanks to Michael Eastman, Barbara Rogers, Gerald and Marion, Gareth Thomas, Arthur Vincent, Den and Joy Harris, Mo, Margaret, ECUM Committee, John Vincent and UTU, my special friend Mel, and my special Steves. I dedicate this piece in gratitude to my wonderful father, Bill Weatherly, who taught me how to love and be kind to all those I met along life's way

John Vincent

WITH DIRTY HANDS

1. Repairing The Walls

"Reading the Bible with Dirty hands" is the slightly illogical but striking theme of the July 2001 Sheffield meeting of the Institute for British Liberation Theology.   On Wednesday July 11th, the Institute are taking an afternoon break, to walk from the Urban Theology Unit in Abbeyfield Road, down through the old Burngreave Cemetery and to the bottom of Burngreave Road, to Spital Hill.   There, we have a brief walk around the Burngreave Ashram. The Ashram Community Trust purchased these rambling premises in January 2001, but so far have not had the money to get them going in more than frail, skeleton order.

The aim of the Burngreave Ashram was stated clearly enough in the initial "Prospectus":

> The Ashram Community Trust has the opportunity to purchase an extraordinary complex of shops, basement, flat, offices, dance studio, workshop space and 2-storey works.   It is situated in a prominent location on the main road through Sheffield's northern inner city, alongside ethnic and local shops, restaurants, DSS, library, housing office, and local advice centres.   Spital Hill is the hub of Sheffield's most deprived and decayed multi-racial inner city.   The coming of the Burngreave Ashram is seen as a significant addition to the range of community and personal outlets needed to help the regeneration of this long-time blighted area.

> The Burngreave Ashram will be an umbrella complex, within which a variety of community facilities and services will be provided.   The Residential Community will bring a household of people who will contribute to the life of the area.   New Roots shop will provide a "healthy living" base in the area,where wholefood, fresh produce, real bread, lunch pasties, vegetarian and vegan products will be available.   The Dance

Studio and the offices will be used as local community needs emerge.

So, since January 2001, the small group of Sheffield Branch Ashram Community members, plus three or four other local people, have been tip-toeing into the area, "spying out the land" (Num 13:16-17), then "walking up and down in it" (Zech 10:12) and starting to "repair the ruins of the house" (Ezra 9:9). We are the children of Israel going into the hostile "promised land", the people returning from exile to rebuild the derelict city, the community of the end-time, setting up an outpost of the coming *shalom*! Our "philosophy we state as follows:

> The idea behind the Burngreave Ashram is to provide a complex, an emporium, for the inspiration and animation of local community groups, projects, activities and industry. The philosophy of the Ashram Community Trust is that it is ecumenical and radical, within the broad spectrum of Christianity, but without any denominational or doctrinal restriction....Burngreave Ashram will seek to be a welcoming, facilitating partner with local individuals and groups in developing appropriate services and spaces, while at the same time separately continuing its own life as an Ashram Community Branch/ Project, with regular open community gatherings.

As with our biblical forebears, it all comes down to the long, slow task of repairing, rebuilding, redesigning, adapting, decorating and cleaning. The work goes by fits and starts, as the money becomes available, or people's voluntary commitments make possible, or temporary interest drifts in our direction. Conceivably, we will get grants – Burngreave has £60 million just agreed as a New Deal for Communities. But how, and with what partners, and on what terms there might be money remains to be seen. At present it's just the "dirty hands" of clearing rubble, construction, painting, sweeping up and scrubbing. None of us have any particular skills in any of these things. We come with clean hands. But they do not remain clean for long.

We said from the beginning that there would be some kind of Sunday Lunch Gathering, where we bring and share a meal, and read and share stories and ideas that will build up our vision, sustain our commitment, and confirm our solidarity. There, those with dirty hands come to share the sustaining stories and mutuality of the Christian way. So we announced:

> The heart of the Burngreave Ashram developments is seen as the Sunday Lunch Gathering. We are a Gathering of people

influenced by the life and ministry of Jesus. The variety of people attending the Gathering will take responsibility for arranging and leading various parts of the occasion – music, song, Gospel reading, other readings, local community concerns, meditation, prayers. In addition, we invite a speaker who will open up a topic and invite discussion. People of all faiths and spiritualities, and none, are welcome to come and join us, and to share their insights. The Gathering commences at 12.30 with a Bring and Share Meal. The various elements of the Gathering should last until around 2.15.

2. Showing His Hands

In this context, from the first Gathering on April 29th, I have found myself, somewhat unexpectedly for a persistent lecturer and writer on Mark's Gospel, drawn to a weekly reflection on the resurrection stories of John 20.

I could have begun with the women at the tomb, I suppose, in John 20:1-18. But I felt drawn to the events which John records for the first Easter Day evening. There we were, meeting in the midst of strange territory, through the usually heavily padlocked gate, up the concrete steps, and through two doors into the old dance studio – looking at each other somewhat qiizzically, tired, unprepared, hardly holding on to the vision, separated from all that we had known or been confident with. A bit like those first disciples:

> On the evening of that day, the first day of the week, the doors were shut where the disciples were, for fear of the Jewish authorities. Then Jesus came and stood among them, and said to them, "Peace be with you". (John 20:19)

A bit like those first disciples, we looked at each other. Who are we? Are we still together? Galileans, what are we doing here in Jerusalem? What can we make of our new place? What will this new place make of us? What is *happening* to us? Will we ever be the same again? And what about the powerful authorities – the drug dealers, the gangs, the ethnic groups – out in the street?

And beyond that, like those first disciples, there were great, yawning unanswerables. Who will join us? Will anyone join us? What do we have to do? What will we end up like? No answer came , except Jesus' "Well, it's the same for you as it was for me. You've got the Father and the Spirit, and the power. I never had anything you don't have" (John 20:21-23). Like them, we didn't believe it. But we're still there, dumbfounded, with no more appearances meanwhile, the following week:

> Eight days later, his disciples were again in the house, and Thomas was with them. The doors were shut, but Jesus came and stood among them, and said, "Peace be with you". Then he said to Thomas, "Put your finger here, and see my hands. And put out your hand, and place it in my side." (John 20:26-27)

The marks on the hand and the wound in the side! Of course! Every piece of discipleship, every action of the divine Kingdom, every practice of servant ministry or political prophecy or community formation, must begin here. The hands and the side!

As I said, we had to pull out the builders, long before the shop was finished. All the builders' scaffolding and equipment – and dirt! – was still there. And we said, Maybe we have to go back, and not produce a lovely new shop. Maybe that might have looked too good, too professional, too middle class. Let's just get ourselves and a few friends in there, on Saturdays, and do bits of cleaning and painting, by ourselves.

So, for the Saturdays of June, we were in there, four or five of us, doing jobs and getting our hands dirty, and talking to passers by who would peer in or ask us what we were doing. And we were able to say that we were trying to get something going. Showing them our hands. Saying, reach here, and see our hands.

And the side? No lance has pierced us. But our heart is, kind of, broken – the blood and the water (John 19:34). Yet there is a fear still among us. Will the gangs leave us alone, because we are so vulnerable? Will the drug dealers turn a blind eye at us because of our obvious foolishness? We wake up at night, sometimes, in fear. We close the doors every time we go in. And our heart grieves – our side is pierced.

3. Back to Galilee

Then on Sunday July 8th, it is the Community Festival in Abbeyfield Park. We have a table, and take our pasties and samosas and wholefoods and real bread and some fruit. And we say to the people, "Next Saturday, and every Saturday, we'll be open at Spital Hill. Will you come and join us? Buy from us, or even help us? And if you can make things and want to sell them, come and have a table there, alongside ours."

Going out into Abbeyfield Park is like the Disciples going back to Galilee:

> After this, Jesus revealed himself again to the disciples by the Sea of Tiberias. Simon Peter said, "I am going fishing". They said to him, "We will go with you". (John 21:1, 3)

At last we're away from the upper room with closed doors. Lets go fishing! Who knows who might be out there, waiting for us? We'll sell some samosas, and we might get some disciples! And the fresh air will be good, after the dust and builders' rubble, the paint and the cleaning materials at the shop. We'll go back to the people, where we came from, back to Galilee.

And, who knows, something else might happen:

> Jesus said to them, "Lads, have you caught any fish?" They answered, "No". So he said to them, "Put your nets down on the right, and you will find some". (John 21: 5, 6)

When you're starting a new venture, or opening up a new possibility, for the business of the Kingdom of God, you often spend a lot of time, as they say, "barking up the wrong tree". You can make a bee-line for the sorts of people who might be expected to come and find you – and they don't come at all! You might think your friends are going to be on the left, and they turn out to be on the right!

4. Re-inventing the Good News

At the back of our minds, we are already back in Galilee, as he had appointed for us. (Mark 14:28, 16:7). Every now and then, we look over the elements of our situation and the Gospel calls and we discover what we must be faithful with. So we mull over the mission we had more than a year before:

104

Local Agenda:	Gospel Practice:	First Steps:
Poor health anti-ecological lifestyle early mortality rates	SEEDS GROWING SECRETLY (Mark 4:26-29). Seeds of alternative sustainable life Gospel lifestyle Simplicity and hope	NEW ROOTS Discover allies, Experiment with various sales and uses - So, restore the shop.
Inter-racial conflict Alienation Fear. No residents on street	DISCIPLE COMMUNITY (Mark 1:16-23, 3:14) Two or three – Follow me Church in house Incarnational community	COMMUNITY FLATS Discover likely people, Publicity, Meetings - So restore the flats.
Lack of community No training opportunities Lack of meeting space	OPEN HOUSE (Acts 2:43-47) Food & Fellowship Gathering Gospel discovery Political forum for Radical Christianity	DANCE STUDIO Start Sunday Lunch Gathering Discover interested people Open Community meeting room - So, use the dance studio.
Deprivation Multiple needs Lack of Ministry	JESUS' HOUSE (Mark 2:1-2) Personal Ministries	OFFICE Bases for local workers Contact point Classes and consultation - So, refurbish Offices.
Lack of places for local organisations	POTTER'S HOUSE (Jer 18:2, Acts 4:32-27) People developing potential Gospel style economics	CELLAR Indigenous Craft/Art/Servicing - So, open up Cellar.

Of course, it will not turn out just like this. But these are the gospel pieces we hold in our hands as we try to live with and discover things within the environment and the locality. At least, in all the undertainty, we have plenty of "first steps" to get on with – and not enough people and money to do them! And no-one yet has been called to come and live there – but they will be!

5. Contemporary Gospel

The story I have told is one I could have told on the basis of previous experiences in the Sheffield Inner City Ecumenical Mission. It was very similar when we sold Wesley Hall, Grimesthorpe, and moved thirteen members into the corner shop off-licence on Birdwell Road in 1980. It was similar when the four remaining members sold the Lopham Street Chapel and bought the Furnival Public House in 1996. Indeed, all three were licensed premises – 80 Spital Hill was last used as Pinky's Night Club!

Is there something in this experience of succeeding decline, desertion and death, followed by despair and loneliness and desolation in a new place after the tomb, where then resurrection slowly begins to take place? Is there something in these experiences of practice which mirrors, reflects and continues the experiences of the post-resurrection disciples of Jesus? My interest in all this is also an interest as a persistent student of the Gospels and of Jesus. Faced with the evidence of my practice in ministry, I have to ask, Is this not the appropriate, the proper way to have fellowship today with the odd stories of the Gospel narratives?

The experiences of "walking with the Gospel", of "reading the Gospel with dirty hands", or of a "hands-on Gospel practice" seems to put one alongside the actual experiences of the first disciples in a way which does justice to contemporary Audience Criticism, Reader Response Criticism and Rhetorical Criticism.[1] Moreover, using the resurrection narrative as an accompaniment to discipleship, or a spur to Kingdom activity seems to set one alongside the first disciples, and their practices, in a striking way. It certainly feels more appropriate than the frequent use of the resurrection narratives in other ways – as model for one's "spiritual journey", or an assurance of "eternal life". It was not a spiritual journey, and any relationship to eternal life is nowhere stated.

So, beyond "Imaginative Identification",[2] something more and something decisively more is needed. I describe the 'decisively more' as 'coherence with God's Project'[3]- the project of bringing the presence and new reality of God's Kingdom to specific lives and situations. So the question has to follow the typical Gospel agenda and sequence, as the synoptics especially record them, and ask:

> Where does the Practice not merely resonate as a story with a piece of Gospel story, but actually participate in the same reality or event, but actually participate in the same reality or event – specifically, the Gospel actions of:
>> speaking to people by name
>> dealing with the presenting situation
>> healing the sufferer
>> calling the healed person to new life
>> securing a new future for the victim
>> asserting the new community of the healed
>> challenging the powers that were victimising
>> confronting the critics.

The debate between pieces of Practice – that is, anything going on under the name of Christians, Christianity, or Christian community – has to be – How far, and in what specific ways, are parts of this "good news" being embodied?

Beyond this dynamic, there is also the wider scene in society, of which the personal cameo was representative. Se, we ask further:

> Where does the Practice not merely deal with an individual person or a special situation, but also tackles the social, political and cultural situations which contribute to the oppression – specifically, by
>
>> naming the real oppressors
>> dealing with the social and political situation
>> healing all in a similar state
>> calling communities to wholeness
>> securing new futures for communities
>> creating faith communities of the newly enfranchised
>> tackling the wider economic controllers
>> debating with the critics and media.

The beginnings of this wider societal practice are visible in the New Testament, and occasionally in the Gospels – though the power of a tiny alien sect to alter the temple/Herodian hegemony or the Roman Empire obviously limited this dimension.

6. Gospel from the Underside

Ian Duffield observes that any particular Bible passage can function in varied ways.

(a) in the consideration of what should be done, and how it should be done
(b) during engagement with action
(c) as a matter of reflection after practice.[4]

Each of these "moments" was present in the Burngreave Ashram story just told – the planning, the actual practice, and the reflection.

From the point of view of the Bible as "a book full of stories", one is bound to reflect on the "use" – and non-use – of central stories. Questions like these become inevitable and appropriate:

> Who really needs this story?
> Who has things going on that only make sense in the light of this story?
> Who has happenings which seem most naturally to be able to utilise the words of this story?

Where do there seem to be actions and practice that are coherent with the actions and practice described in this story?
Where are people with dirty hands using this story for solidarity, strengthening and projection?

The argument of this present book is surely that the "underside" has an advantage over other contexts when it comes to having practice that coheres with Gospel practice. We recreate the Gospel in our own time by repeating bits of the actions of the Gospels in our own contexts. We need the variety of Gospel stories to discover which stories we are being called upon to re-enact, but also which contexts, problems, issues, people and communities these stories belong to.

The point is not, therefore, just to have a *reading* of the Gospels in our context. It is more an "urban *hearing*" of the Gospels that we need.[5] But now I want to say that it is a contextual *re-enactment* of the Gospels that is the point. "Imaginative Identification" must lead on to Imaginative Reconfiguration, Imaginative Recapitulation, Imaginative *Reprise*. This is what I now want to argue for. In the terms of Gospel scholarship, it is an "Outworkings", or a "Gospel Practice Criticism".[6]

So, our contributors see elements in the social and cultural mores, and the actual practice of inner city or working class congregations which go naturally with the bible study.[7] Hence the methods of Jenny Richardson[8] or the re-membering of the story by the people, as told by Janet Lees[9] The Bible as a supporter of human subversion, as Tim Gorringe describes it,[10] comes into its own, and functions authentically, almost by accident, in the black churches, as described by Joe Aldred and Garnet Parris,[11] or in the lives of the less than "successful" as per Ann Weatherly[12]

This rediscovery of the Bible from the Underside, from the Margins, from the Excluded, from the Poor, has been recently highlighted in the work of Joerg Reiger from Dallas, who was with us and spoke to us at the 2000 Institute on his book *Remember the Poor*.[13] Joerg Rieger's prime concern is with the implications of the Bible "rediscovery" for theology. Indeed, contemporary Gospel-style Practice re-opens the whole question of what Christianity could be. Will conventional Christianity ever abandon its worship of "clean hands and a pure heart" (Psalm 24:4)? The Gospel practice of Jesus has a contrary blessedness: dirty hands and a broken heart – the beginning of good news for the underside.

7. Theologies from Practice

Beyond this, the build-up of stories of contemporary radical Christian witness and ministry insight hopefully begin actually to change theology. This wider question, I began to reflect upon in *Hope from the City*, where I tell stories of practice in the Sheffield Mission branches, and then rehearse the way in which particular Gospel stories are used to confirm, expand or explain them. I comment:

> There is hope from the city for tired Christians and even Theologians! Here are people who take the way of Christian discipleship as a way meant to be lived in every part of their lives – *who* they see themselves as, *where* they become incarnate, *with whom* they place themselves, for *what* they give their lives. There is hope for the future of Christianity if it becomes again a radical alternative of costly and relevant discipleship, lived out in love and faith wherever there is human need. The little communities and people of the inner cities are signs of hope for all.[14]

Hence the questions arising from this seem to be:

> What theology derives from this Gospel/Bible provoked action?
> What God could be predicated from this apparent incarnation-consistent practice?

These questions can be set in a "hermeneutical circle". Following the models of Christine Jones and Ian Duffield[15], this would go from street to reflection to street again, but with the new, Bible-inspired street practice providing its own new Bible reading and new Theology.

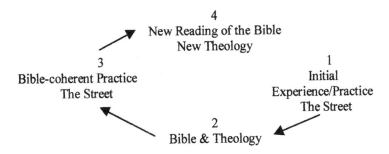

4
New Reading of the Bible
New Theology

3
Bible-coherent Practice
The Street

1
Initial
Experience/Practice
The Street

2
Bible & Theology

The key to the whole is the "Bible-Coherent Practice".

109

The full implications of this emphasis on the priority of Gospel-coherent practice remain to be discovered. I think it side-steps the frustrating question about where you are supposed to start – with experience, or gospel, or situation, or practice. All of these are vital parts of it. But which way the "hermeneutical circle" includes each of them, and in what order, hardly matters. The Gospel-coherent practice is the central element, the vital element, the point of it all.

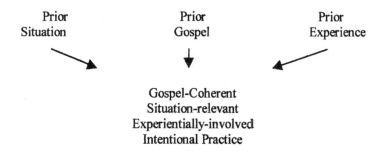

Prior Situation   Prior Gospel   Prior Experience

Gospel-Coherent
Situation-relevant
Experientially-involved
Intentional Practice

Without the intentional practice, situation remains only the neutral scene or stage, however fascinating its stories and dynamics. Without the intentional practice, Gospel remains a mere hearing, not doing (Luke 8:21, James 1:23), a Kingdom of words not in power (1 Corinthians 4:20). Without the intentional practice, experience remains the self-bound interiority of self-fulfilment, divorced of the redeeming mystery of discovery (cf Mark 8:35). "Be doers of the word", says James (1:22).

If, in our next volume, we try to record "Theologies from Practice", does this not mean that there is in fact a "canon" of practice, or a "selective canon" of certain practices, as there is a "selective canon" of certain biblical passages, in all experiential and theological readings of scripture? How will we know *whose* or *what* practice, and the theological reflection thereon, gets into our collection?

I fancy that we already have some hunches about the answers to these questions. Liberation Theology's prime commitment is to certain practice. Theology is the second - or twenty-second - act.

[1] John Vincent, Hope From the City. Epworth Press 2000, pp. 39-40

[2] "Imaginative Identification", Epworth Review, 23.3, September 1996, pp. 14-20

[3] John Vincent, Hope From the City. Epworth Press 2000, p. 159 and *passim*.

[4] Ian K. Duffield in this volume, p.75

[5] "An Urban Hearing of the Gospel", Gospel from the City. ed. Rowland & Vincent, UTU, 1997, pp. 105-116

[6] "Outworkings. A Gospel Practice Criticism", *Expository Times*, forthcoming.

[7] Ian K. Duffield, above, p. 69.

[8] Jenny Richardson in this volume, esp. pp. 24 – 31.

[9] Janet Lees in this volume, esp. pp. 35 – 37.

[10] Tim Gorringe in this volume, pp. 44 - 51

[11] Joe Aldred and Garnet Parris in this volume, pp. 52 - 65

[12] Ann Weatherly in this volume, pp.88 - 99

[13] Joerg Reiger, Remember the Poor. Trinity Press International, 1998; also see God and the Excluded. Fortress Press, 2001.

[14] John Vincent, Hope From the City. Epworth Press 2000, p. 162

[15] Christine Jones, "Vortex Theology", in Ian Duffield, Christine Jones and John Vincent, Crucibles: Creating Theology at UTU. UTU 2000, pp. 6-16, p. 11

CONTRIBUTORS

Bishop Joe Aldred is currently the Executive Director of the Centre for Black and White Christian Partnership, Selly Oak, Birmingham and a bishop in the Church of God of Prophecy. He holds a Sheffield/UTU MMin and is a PhD candidate.

Andrew Davey was vicar of St Luke's, North Peckham, and is now Secretary for Community and Urban Affairs at the Anglican Board of Social Responsibility, London. His theological background includes UTU, Sheffield, and Tamil Nadu, India.

Ian K. Duffield is Vicar of Walkley, Sheffield. He has been a supervisor for UTU postgraduate in-service degrees in ministry (MMin/DMin) for the last sixteen years. He edited *Urban Christ* (UTU, 1997) and was a contributor to *Crucibles* ((UTU, 2000)

Tim Gorringe is an Anglican Priest and the St Luke's Foundation Professor of Theological Studies in the University of Exeter. Recent books include *Karl Barth: Against Hegemony* (Oxford, 1999)

Janet Lees is a speech therapist and a URC minister. She combines these two aspects of ministry in the Sheffield Inner City Ecumenical Mission in a project called 'Let's Talk', based at St James URC. She is also minister at Shiregreen URC.

Garnet Parris studied theology at St. John's College, Nottingham, Nottingham University, and London Bible College. He co-ordinates the work of the African Diaspora in Europe, and has pastored in Trinidad.

Bridget Rees was a founder member of Women in Theology. After being an Anglican Education Advisor and Christian Aid area organiser, in 1997 she became Director of the Mirfield Centre. She is now Director of Mission in Bradford Diocese.

Jenny Richardson lives in inner city Sheffield. She is Chief Executive of Unlock, formerly the Evangelical Urban Training Project, which resources urban Christians, and has a particular interest in the work of Paulo Friere.

Christopher Rowland is Professor of New Testament Theology in the University of Oxford. He is author of *Christian Origins* and *Radical Christianity*, and co-author of *Liberating Exegesis*.

John Vincent is Honorary Lecturer and MPhil/PhD Supervisor for the Sheffield University doctoral programme in Contextual, Urban and Liberation Theologies at UTU. His most recent book is *Hope From the City*, (Epworth Press, 2000).

Ann Weatherly has opened her home to those in need for 18 years. She edits and designs '*Urban Bulletin*' and CURBS Project packs as well as being Parish Clerk and writing a book.

Ruth Sharples Weston has lived, with her young family in inner city Bradford for the last nine years. Amongst other things she is a worker for Unlock, and is part of a group setting up a 'house of prayer and interfaith dialogue' in Bradford.

CHRONICLE

THE INSTITUTE FOR BRITISH LIBERATION THEOLOGY

Twenty-six people attended the Institute in July 1999 in Sheffield. Volume 3 of this series was introduced, and seven of the contributors introduced their contributions. The major theme of the Institute was "Bible and Practice", with participative Bible Studies led by Jenny Richardson, Chris Rowland and Bridget Rees, and individual studies introduced by David Rhodes, Tim Gorringe, Ian Duffield, Ann Weatherly, Janet Lees and Jane Grinonneau. This fourth volume of the British Liberation Theology series contains revised versions of most of the contributions, plus three added since.

The 2000 Institute met for a weekend, 14 – 16 July 2000, jointly with the British Black Theology Forum. After sharing stories on the Friday evening, the speakers on the Saturday were Delroy Hall on "Black Men's and Authentic Identity", Isadore Aitken on "Seek the welfare of all in the city", Joseph Basappa on "Asian and Dalit Theology", Robert Beckford on *Dread and Pentecostalism* (A launch of his SPCK book), Inderjit Bhogal on "Negotiating Identities" and Anthony Reddie on "Education and Conscientization". The evening consisted of responses to the day from Institute members, and separate planning meetings. On the Sunday, Joerg Rieger of Southern Methodist University, Dallas, introduced his book *Remember the Poor* (TPI, 1999)

The subject for the Institute of Tuesday – Thursday, 9-11 July 2002 is planned to be "Theology From Practice", featuring the wide variety of experiences, contexts and communities in which contemporary liberation practice occurs in Britain. Offers of contributions are invited and should be addressed to the Joint Convenors, Bridget Rees and John Vincent, Urban Theology Unit, 210 Abbeyfield Road, Sheffield S4 7AZ. Plans between the July Institutes are made by the Management Committee listed on p. 2.

BRITISH LIBERATION THEOLOGIES NOW

At the October 1999 Consultation at Wistaston, Mike Simpson and Joan Sharples were thanked for their secretarial work in the six bi-annual BLT Consultations, 1989 – 1999. The story is in *Liberation Spirituality*, volume 3 of this series, pp. 74-94. At the October 1999 meeting, it was agreed to continue the Consultation, with a new title: "BLT Now"", and a new coordinating group, consisting of Tim Presswood, Bridget Rees and Joan Sharples. The new name is intending to reflect "the variety of liberation theologies which hold each other in creative tension within that creative tension we call Britain".

The 2000 Consultation was held at Wistaston on 24-26 November. On the Friday evening, members shared "Sustenance – What Has and Does Sustain Us?", and the Saturday was spent in groups, "Sharing Stories and Discerning Issues". Four questions were addressed:

What is there about the gospel that frees us/ has freed us?
What has the Lord been calling us to do?
What resistances have we encountered?
What is the Lord calling us to do here and now?

Inderjit Bhogal, Ian Fraser and Margaret Nolan then led a Plenary. On Sunday, Bridget Rees led us through "Taking, Thanking, Breaking and Sharing" into a final session of Evaluating, Dreaming, Talking, Worshipping and Planning. The next consultation will be 15-17 November, 2000.

UTU SUMMER INSTITUTES

The British Liberation Theology Institute in July forms part of a series of Summer occasions at UTU. Details are as follows:

1. The Forum for British Black Theology
The Forum for British Black Theology is an annual meeting of workers and writers of British Black and Asian Theologies. Contributions are invited, which may become part of a proposed Journal. The Forum takes place at UTU in Sheffield. Future dates are Saturday 14th July 2001, Saturday 13th July 2002 and July dates in subsequent years. Enquiries to the Chair: Revd Inderjit Bhogal, 210 Abbeyfield Road, Sheffield S4 7AZ

2. The Institute for Socio-Biblical Studies
The Institute for Socio-Biblical Studies is convened by Emeritus Professor John Rogerson at UTU each July. Speakers include John Rogerson, Professor Philip Davies and other members of the Sheffield University Biblical Studies Department. Usually, the Wednesday is devoted to Old Testament presentations, and the Thursday to New Testament presentations, which recently included Professor Chris Rowland (2000) and Dr Ivor Jones (2001). Dates are 4 - 5 July 2001 and 3 - 4 July 2002. Details from UTU.

3. The Institute for Urban Theology

The Institute for Urban Theology, convened by Ian K. Duffield and John Vincent, reports and resources the distinctive development of Urban Theology. The subject for 2001 meeting is "Theology from Urban Mission", with contributions from US colleagues who are also attending a five-day Urban Mission Exploration. The dates are Wednesday – Thursday, 18 – 19 July 2001, and 17 – 18 July 2002. Please write to UTU for more information.

4. Green Theology Forum

A Green Theology Forum, convened by Christine Jones, usually takes place. The dates for 2002 are Monday – Tuesday, 8 – 9 July.

Theological students, ministers and lay people are invited to come to the whole July Programme at UTU, joining with overseas visitors who attend at this time, including other visits. Dates are 4 – 19 July 2001 and 3 – 18 July 2002.

OTHER COURSES

1. The Doctoral Programme in Contextual, Urban and Liberation Theologies

A MPhil/PhD course in Contextual, Urban and Liberation Theologies, with Dr John Vincent as Supervisor, and an Associate Supervisor from the Biblical Studies Department of Sheffield University, uses the Urban Theology Unit as base. Degrees are awarded by Sheffield University. Groups of candidates meet quarterly at UTU for 3-day periods over the first two years, of the part-time course, then single days. Enquiries to: Dr John Vincent, Urban Theology Unit, 210 Abbeyfield Road, Sheffield S4 7AZ.

2. The Urban Theology Collective

Arising from the Urban Theology Programme at St Deiniol's in Autumn 1999, there is now an annual Urban Theology Collective, the first meeting of which in December 2000 revised the publication *Faithfulness in the City*. The Collective for the year 2001 will be held on Monday – Friday, 3rd – 7th December at St Deiniols. Individuals offer short presentations and people open up ideas. Expected themes are:

   Theological Reflection on Regeneration
   Developments in Urban Ministry and Theology Training
   Urban Mission and Urban Theology Developments

Details from Andrew Davey or John Vincent, or from the Warden, Revd Peter Francis, St Deiniols Library, Hawarden, Flintshire CH5 3DF.

RECENT PUBLICATIONS

The Cambridge Companion to Liberation Theology   Ed. Christopher Rowland.   Cambridge University Press, 1999.   Discussions of the global background to our work in Britain.

Laurie Green's *The Impact of the Global: An Urban Theology* was published by UTU as New City Special 13, in May 2000.   Price £3.00.

Inderjit Bhogal's *A Table for All*, Penistone Publications, 2000, marks his year as President of the Methodist Conference, 2000 – 2001, and contains his Presidential Address and his "faith journey".   Price £3.00.

"Developing Contextual Theologies", by John Vincent, Epworth Revie. w, July 2000, compares Contextual, Liberation and Urban Theologies. Reprinted with essays by Ian K. Duffield and Christine Jones in *Crucibles: Creating Theology at UTU*, UTU New City Special 14, 2000.   Price £2.00.

FUTURE PUBLICATIONS

Radical Voices on the Bible: The first volume in this series, edited by Ian K. Duffield and Robin Pagan, is now expected in September 2001, published by UTU in the "People's Bible Study" series.   It is on the Sermon on the Mount – *Jesus' Radical Torah*.

A Radical Christian Reader, edited by Chris Rowland and Andrew Bradstock, with contents widely discussed with colleagues and friends, is to be published by Blackwell's, Oxford, this coming winter.

Andrew Davey's first book, *Local and Global: Urbanisation and Globalisation* is to be published by SPCK in Winter 2001.

British Black and Asian Theology, edited by Inderjit Bhogal and Lerleen Willis, announced for 2000, is planned as a separate publication, in the future.

Faithfulness in the City, edited by John Vincent.   Publisher to be announced. The two-month programme on Urban Theology, led by John Vincent at St Deiniol's Library, Hawarden in October – November 1999, brought around 60 urban practitioners for short or long stays.   This volume contains sixteen pieces of story and testimonies of "People and Communities", followed by "Reflections and Discernments" by Andrew Davey, Michael Northcott, Ian K. Duffield, Stuart Jordan and John Vincent.